THE MARSHALL CAVENDISH
☆ ☆ ☆ ILLUSTRATED ☆ ☆ ☆
ENCYCLOPEDIA OF
WORLD WAR II

VOLUME 8

THE MARSHALL CAVENDISH
☆ ☆ ☆ ILLUSTRATED ☆ ☆ ☆
ENCYCLOPEDIA OF

WORLD WAR II

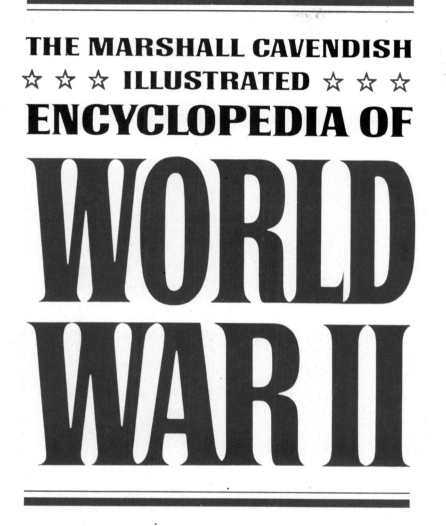

Based on the original text by
Lieutenant Colonel Eddy Bauer

CONSULTANT EDITOR

Brigadier General James L. Collins, Jr., U.S.A.

CHIEF OF MILITARY HISTORY,
DEPARTMENT OF THE ARMY

MARSHALL CAVENDISH CORPORATION/NEW YORK

CONTENTS

Editorial Director: Brian Innes
Editor-in-chief; Brigadier Peter Young, D.S.O., M.C., M.A.
Managing Editor: Richard Humble
Editor: Christopher Chant
Art Editor: Jim Bridge

CHAPTER 72
The Long Agony

At the headquarters of the Soviet 62nd Army (Lieutenant-General V. I. Chuikov), defending Stalingrad, the officer who kept the army's war diary made the following entries on September 14, 1942:

"0730: the enemy has reached Academy Street.

0740: 1st Battalion 38th Mechanised Brigade is cut off from our main forces.

0750: fighting has flared up in the sector of Mamaev-Kurgan hill and in the streets leading to the station.

0800: the station is in enemy hands.

0840: the station is in our hands.

0940: the station has been retaken by the enemy.

1040: the enemy has reached Pushkin Street, 500 yards from the Army's Battle Headquarters.

1100: two regiments of infantry supported by 30 tanks are moving towards the Technical Institution."

These brief notes, taken from the *Great Patriotic War*, are sufficient without further comment to show how bitter was the struggle between the Russians and the Germans, first in the streets, then in the ruins of Stalingrad. This struggle was now in its third month.

On September 14, weakened by the battles in the great curve of the Don, the 62nd Army had only 50,000 fighting men left. On the following night, however, the 13th Guards Division (Major-General Rodimtzev) was sent across the Volga in reinforcement and this enabled Lieutenant-General Chuikov to retake Mamaev-Kurgan hill. Two other infantry divisions; an infantry brigade, and an armoured brigade also crossed the river on ferries to take part in the defence of Stalingrad.

These reinforcements did not, however, prevent the German 6th Army, powerfully supported by *Luftflotte* IV, from scoring victories. By September 20 they had

▽ *A soldier takes a final pull on his cigarette as German infantry wait the order to advance from their start line. In the workers' suburbs, the fighting was comparatively easy as most of the buildings were wood and could be burned or blasted by tanks or aircraft.*

reached the banks of the Volga, slightly downstream of the station which they had finally occupied. This cut off the 62nd Army on its left from the 64th (Major-General M. S. Shumilov), and trapped it against the river for some 15 miles.

Russian street fighting tactics

There is no doubt that in the battle for Stalingrad, Paulus had numerical and *matériel* superiority, but if he could not take advantage of it as he did on the Don, it was because the nature of the street fighting deprived him of most of the advantages of his tanks and planes. In his memoirs, Chuikov, later a Marshal, gives a clear indication of this: success "did not depend on strength, but on ability, skill, daring, guile. Buildings split up enemy formations like break-waters, forcing them to follow the line of the streets. That is why we clung to the most solid ones, with small units capable of all-round defence. These buildings allowed us to set up centres of resistance from which the defenders mowed down the Nazis with their automatic weapons."

In this connection it must be recalled that the Russians had followed more closely than the Germans the fighting between the Spanish Nationalists and Republicans in December 1936 in the outer suburbs and, especially, the University City in Madrid. Experience had shown that large, modern concrete buildings were all but proof against medium artillery fire. And there were many such buildings in Stalingrad, especially large factory buildings, of which Marshal Chuikov said that their "solid construction in metal and concrete and the development of their underground installations allowed prolonged and bitter resistance".

At the request of Paulus, Colonel-General von Richthofen, the commander of *Luftflotte* IV, strove to make up for the lack of artillery by heavy bombing. But the only effect of this was to create enormous amounts of rubble in the streets, which prevented the use of armour, and the German engineers of the time had no bulldozers to clear such rubble away

△ *General Chuikov with some staff officers in one of his command posts. He was forced to move his headquarters, but he tried to keep to the west bank of the Volga since he felt that this would help to sustain his men's morale. It also added conviction to his slogan "For us there is no land across the Volga."*
▷ *General Paulus with his staff on the outskirts of the city. The 6th Army, which had driven so swiftly across the steppes of southern Russia, would bog down in the streets of Stalingrad.*

under enemy fire. This was the lesson of experience, but let us note in passing that the Western Allies made the same mistakes both at Cassino and in Normandy.

The German tanks themselves were split up into units of some 15 to 20, but these were prevented from using the range of their guns in the streets, whereas the Russians, in attic windows, cellars, and manholes were able to attack them at a range of a few yards with Molotov cocktails, anti-tank grenades, and 14.5-mm anti-tank rifles, which would have been no good in open country.

The German infantry, moreover, was no better off than its comrades in the Panzers for, Chuikov writes, "the defenders of Stalingrad let the tanks come within range of their guns and anti-tank rifles, and this, at the same time, kept the infantry away from the tanks so that the enemy's normal order of battle was upset. The infantry were wiped out separately as the tanks went ahead of them. And without infantry the tanks were not much good on their own: they were stopped and suffered heavy losses when they pulled back."

In street fighting, rifles, machine guns, and sub-machine guns came into their own, but mention must also be made of the marksmen who, with their semi-automatic rifles fitted with telescopic sights, decimated German detachments.

Hitler's directive of April 5, 1942 had left open the question as to whether Stalingrad should be taken or whether Germany should be content with wiping it out as a centre of war production and of communications. Did Hitler see in Stalingrad a symbol? Or did the elimination of this Soviet bridgehead on the west bank of the Volga seem to him necessary for the successful outcome of the operations then taking place in the Caucasus? We do not know. What is certain, however, is that Paulus received an unequivocal order to complete the conquest of the city at whatever cost. To help him, five battalions of sappers were dispatched to him by air.

Factory to factory combat

This gave new impetus to the attack, whilst increased support was given by the Stukas of the Luftflotte's VIII *Fliegerkorps*. The Orlovka salient was reduced, then, concentrating on a front of two and a half miles, the 305th and the 389th Divisions,

together with the 14th Panzer Division, hurled themselves on to the great industrial complexes known as the "Dzerzinsky" and the "Barricades" on October 14. For the 62nd Army this was a day of crises and severe tests, as its war diary shows:

"0800: enemy attack with tanks and infantry. Battle raging over whole front.

0930: enemy attack on Tractor Factory repulsed. Ten tanks on fire in factory yard.

1000: tanks and infantry crush the 109th Regiment of the 37th Division (Major-General Zheludov).

1130: left flank of 524th Infantry Regiment of the 95th Division smashed in. Some 50 tanks are rolling up the Regiment's positions.

1150: enemy has occupied stadium at Tractor Factory. Our units cut off inside and fighting their way out.

1200: commander of 117th Regiment, Guards Major Andreyev, killed.

1220: radio message from unit of 416th Regiment from hexagonal block of flats: 'Surrounded; have water and cartridges; will die rather than surrender.'

1230: Stukas attack General Zheludov's H.Q. General in his collapsed shelt-

△ *A Stuka pulls out over a burning fuel dump. When Chuikov discovered that the Luftwaffe would only bomb forward positions when there was a clear gap of no-man's land, he urged his troops to reduce this distance to hand grenade range. This meant that it was difficult for the Germans to neutralise buildings in the town which had been turned into strongpoints, for fear of hitting their own men.*

er without communications. We are liaising with elements of his Division.

1310: two shelters collapse at Army H.Q. An officer trapped by legs in rubble. Can't free him.

1525: Army H.Q. guard now fighting in battle.

1635: Lieutenant-Colonel Ustinov, commanding infantry regiment, asks for artillery fire on his H.Q. He is surrounded by enemy with submachine guns."

From the opposing side, Major Grams offers us confirmation of the terrible battles of October, in which he took part as commander of a motorised battalion in the 14th Panzer Division. In his history of this famous unit he writes: "It was an appalling and exhausting battle at both ground level and underground in the ruins, the cellars, the drains of this large city. Man to man, hero to hero. Our tanks clambered over great mountains of rubble and plaster, their tracks screeching as they drove their way through ruined workshops, opening fire at point-blank range in narrow streets blocked by fallen masonry or in the narrow factory yards. Several of our armoured colossi shook visibly or blew up as they ran over mines."

The worst thing for the Germans to bear, according to Grams, was the fact that every night hundreds of ferries brought in reinforcements across the Volga and there was no way of stopping them. In fact, during the night of October 17–18, the Soviet 138th Division (Colonel I. I. Lyudnikov) arrived at a very opportune moment to bolster up the defence of the "Barricades" factory sector. LI Corps (General von Seydlitz-Kurzbach) had occupied the Tractor Factory itself, and had even reached the river bank but, faced with the Russians' continuous and insurmountable resistance, their attacks petered out, as previous ones had done.

Meanwhile Hitler, who was in Munich to celebrate the eighteenth anniversary of the abortive 1923 *Putsch* among the faithful, considered the battle for Stalingrad, and with it the war in Russia, as won. "I wished," he shouted in his raucous voice, "to get to the Volga and at a certain time and a certain place. It happens to be named after Stalin himself. But do not think that that is why I directed our efforts against it; it could have had quite a different name. No. It is because this is a particularly important place. This is where 30 million tons of traffic comes to

be sorted out, including some nine million tons of petrol. This is where all the cereals from the huge regions of the Ukraine and the Kuban' pass through on their way to the north. This is where manganese ore is sent. This is where there are huge transshipment facilities. I wanted to take it and let me tell you, for we are modest, we have it!" This message had more effect on the party members crowded into the Munich Beer Cellar than on the fighters on the Stalingrad front. They knew what the real truth was, and it was them Hitler now told to "finish it off". It also shows

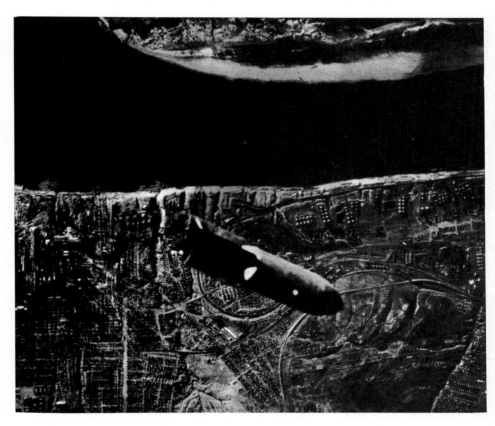

that the Führer did not know–or pretended not to know–about the railway linking Astrakhan' and Saratov, bypassing Stalingrad and the Volga's great western bend.

More German advances

Yet on November 10, the German LI Corps, still fighting in the breach, renewed its assaults with armour and sappers; at the cost of incredible effort it succeeded in isolating from the rest of the Russian 62nd Army the defenders of the "Barricades", whose courage still remained steadfast, and in overrunning the workers' quarters attached to the "Red October" factory. They got inside the factory

◁ *A Russian patrol in the ruins of once populous Stalingrad.*
◁▽ *Colonel Lyudnikov, whose division at one time held a bridgehead on the west bank only a mile square. The Russians had the advantage of secure artillery positions and airstrips on the east bank, but supplies and reinforcements had to be ferried across by night, and this became increasingly difficult as winter started to send ice floes down the Volga.*

△ *A heavy bomb descends on the "tennis racquet", a Russian bridgehead six miles square held by Chuikov's 62nd Army. The nickname for the area was derived from the circular shape of the railway marshalling yards. Overleaf: Russian troops prepare to cross the Volga in this painting by V. K. Dmitrievsky.*

The fighting in Stalingrad put great pressure on the junior N.C.O.s and sub-sections of both armies. A determined leader could turn a solid building into a fortress, or lead a patrol through the sewers and gullies that led from the river into the centre of the city.

△ *A Russian patrol clambers through a maze of shattered buildings.*

▽ *A Soviet 76-mm gun fires through the dust and smoke of a street battle. Each side used artillery in direct support to batter down the factories and department stores that had been fortified.*

itself, but then the attack ground to a halt. The 6th Army had worn itself out: its infantry companies were down to 80 or even 60 men, and the three divisions of its XIV Panzer Corps had only 199 tanks left of which many were inferior Czech types. The situation on the other side had also worsened considerably. On the west bank of the Volga the Russian 62nd Army only had 300 to 1,000 yards behind it. The river was beginning to bring down ice-floes large enough to prevent supplies or reinforcements from crossing. The fact still remains, however, that by now Chuikov knew secretly that he had won a sufficient margin of time, albeit a small one, for Russia, and that within ten days or so the enemy would have something else to think about.

Some of the famous units of the Red Army which distinguished themselves in the defence of Stalingrad have already been mentioned. To these must also be added the 112th and the 308th Divisions, commanded respectively by Colonels I. Zh. Ermolkin and L. N. Gurtiev. Mindful of the soldier in the front line, we quote the tribute to this gigantic struggle by Marshal Eremenko, then in command of the Stalingrad Front.

"The epic of Stalingrad brought out particularly the high and noble qualities of the Soviet people and their heroic army: fervent patriotism, devotion to the Communist cause, fighting comradeship between soldiers of all nationalities, inflexible courage and self-sacrifice, unshakable firmness in defence, forceful bravery in attack, constant liaison and unfailing help between the front and rear areas, brotherhood between soldiers and workers in the factories and the fields. The heroic spirit which has breathed over Stalingrad has borne illustrious testimony to the power of the great Communist Party to guide and inspire our lives and to adapt itself to every circumstance, trustee as it is of the eternal ideas of Lenin."

It will be recalled that Hitler had assumed direct command of Army Group "A" in the Caucasus on September 10. Reduced to some 20 divisions since the transfer of the 4th *Panzerarmee* to Army Group "B", the Germans ended up in late autumn by failing at their last objectives also, just as Stalin had forecast to Winston Churchill. In the Black Sea area, autumn was drawing in and *Gruppe* Ruoff had not got beyond the foothills of the Caucasus. It was thus unable to complete that encircling movement which the Führer had calculated would have given him at best the ports of Tuapse and Sukhumi. The defenders were helped by the forests, the altitude, the rain, and then the snow, all of which showed up the lack of training of the German mountain troops who, however, had been driven very hard. Colonel-General von Kleist had reached Prokhladnyy on the River Terek, which flows out into the Caspian, on August 27. He was no luckier than the others. Held some 50 miles from the Groznyy oilfields, he rallied his III Panzer Corps (General von Mack-

ensen) and swung his attack upstream. This seems to have caught the defence by surprise and he took Nal'chik on October 25 and Alagir on November 5 but failed at Orzhonikidze as he was crossing the Terek. Worse still, this finger that he had rashly thrust into the enemy's positions was all but cut off in counter-attacks, and he nearly lost his 13th Panzer Division. Though it escaped, its near loss put an end to the 1st *Panzerarmee*'s offensive for good and all.

The North Caucasus and the Trans-Caucasus Fronts were now being reinforced week by week, so that on about November 15 the 22 Axis divisions (15 German, six Rumanian, and one Slovak) were opposed by almost 90 major formations, including 37 infantry and eight or nine cavalry divisions, and eight armoured brigades. The tide was about to turn on Germany's effort to secure Caucasian oil.

The Soviet comeback

During their conversations in August, Stalin had told Winston Churchill that he intended to launch a great offensive as winter approached. So during the first fortnight in September Colonel-General A. M. Vasilevsky, replacing the sick Marshal Shaposhnikov as Chief-of-Staff, and his colleague General N. N. Voronov, head of the Red Army's artillery, were sent to the banks of the Volga to deal with the situation. When they returned to *Stavka* it was decided that the forthcoming operation should be in the hands of General G. K. Zhukov. It was expected to engage several Fronts or army groups. Colonel-General Eremenko then had to be relieved of some of his large command, on the South-East and Stalingrad Fronts. The former was renamed the Stalingrad

△ *While the man on the right prepares to give covering fire, a section leader helps one of his men out of a communication trench. All the men are armed with PPSh M 41 sub-machine guns. Though some specialised weapons like flame-throwers were used effectively, the fighting called for mobility and here the sub-machine gun and hand grenade were invaluable.*

△ *A rifleman breaks cover in the snow covered ruins of the city. The Germans never managed to master the art of these small unit tactics, and were even out-classed by the Russian snipers. General Chuikov said that "Every German soldier must be made to feel that he is living under the muzzle of a Russian gun, always ready to treat him to a fatal dose of lead."*

Front and remained under his control; the second became the Don Front, under the command of Lieutenant-General K. K. Rokossovsky.

Originally *Stavka* had allotted only limited objectives to this counter-offensive. Rokossovsky was to attack between the Don and the Volga, link up with the left flank of the armies on the Stalingrad Front and encircle the German 6th Army. The development of this simple early plan into the subsequent triumphant campaign is due to the skill of Colonel-General A. I. Eremenko. On October 6 he got his plan counter-signed by N. S. Khruschev, a member of the Stalingrad Front war council, and sent to Vasilevsky a report in which he reached the following conclusions: "We see the outcome of the mission as the annihilation of the enemy in the Stalingrad sector; from the north powerful groups will drive down to Kalach whilst from the south the 51st and 57th Armies will advance towards Abganerovo and thrust to the north west, that is also towards Kalach."

Eremenko later wrote that "this proposal was based on:
1. firstly the mediocre quality of the troops facing us in the sectors through which we would attempt to drive this would increase our ability to exploit our eventual gains;
2. the enemy's reserves being a long way from the front; and
3. the advantageous type of terrain south of the Don and in the Volga valley lakes."

In fact, a few days previously an attack in the area of the string of lakes extending southwards from Stalingrad had shown the "extreme sensitivity" and the "lack of firmness" of the Rumanian troops in that sector. It is only fair to say that Stalin and Vasilevsky backed up their subordinate's plan at once. This meant that the South-West Front, commanded by Lieutenant-General N. F. Vatutin, would also be involved in the offensive. This front faced the Rumanian 3rd Army and held the deep Serafimovich bridgehead on the south bank of the Don. Thus the attack would develop on a front of 250 miles.

The Russian forces move up

When these decisions had been taken, the next step was to transport men and *matériel* to their concentration areas. The 5th Tank Army (Lieutenant-General P. L. Romanenko) was recalled from the Bryansk Front to become the spearhead of Vatutin's attack. IV Mechanised Corps (Major-General A. G. Kravchenko) and XIII Mechanised Corps (Major-General Tanichikhin) occupied the lake area under strict camouflage precautions as part of Eremenko's front.

In view of the decisive result expected from the campaign, *Stavka* did not hesitate to call upon half its reserve of artillery. Vatutin, Rokossovsky, and Eremenko thus got an additional 75 artillery regiments, bringing their total up to 230, or 13,540 guns and mortars. They were also sent 115 *Katyusha* batteries, with a total of 10,000 launchers. Two air armies were sent to the South-West Front and one each to the Don and Stalingrad Fronts, so that the three fronts had a total of 1,000 planes, including 600 fighters, to call on.

These troop and equipment movements

were usually carried out at night and the strictest orders were given to preserve secrecy. This was also secured by manoeuvres designed to deceive the enemy. Radio operators on the Bryansk Front, for instance, continued to transmit messages for the benefit of enemy listening-posts long after the troops had left the area, and did not rejoin their units on the Don Front until the very last moment.

Can we conclude with Marshal Eremenko that if the German Supreme Command admitted the likelihood of a Russian counter-attack, "it still did not know precisely where or when it would take place"? Eremenko was no doubt basing his opinion on the authority of Colonel-General Jodl, who is said to have declared after the capitulation of the Third Reich: "We had no idea of the gigantic concentrations of Russian forces on the flank of the 6th Army. We did not know in what strength the Soviet troops were massing in this sector. Shortly before the attacks, there was nothing there and suddenly we were struck a massive blow, a blow which was to have far-reaching, even fatal, consequences."

We should remember, however, that at O.K.W. Jodl enjoyed only a partial view of the Eastern Front. From mid-October, both in the German 6th Army and the Rumanian 3rd Army, there was constant concern about enemy activity in the

△ *A Russian sailor in a heroic pose in one of Stalingrad's factory fortresses. Chuikov paid tribute to the Volga flotilla whose guns and ships supported and supplied the troops in the city.*

▽ *Soldiers in the ruined Tractor Factory. This was a focal point for defence in the north of the city, but it fell during the savage assaults late in October.*

bridgeheads he controlled and on the right bank of the Don in the areas of Kletskaya and Serafimovich. Similar signs of movement had been noticed in the sector of the 4th *Panzerarmee*, which extended the right flank of the 6th Army, and Colonel-General Paulus deduced that the enemy was preparing some pincer movement which would be all the more dangerous for the Germans as the Rumanians on the flank were very poorly equipped with anti-tank weapons. He therefore strengthened his left flank by bringing over the Don the armoured units of his 14th Panzer Division into General Strecker's XI Corps, but he could do no more as he had the strictest orders from Hitler to hold Stalingrad at all costs.

Zeitzler proposes a withdrawal

Paulus naturally informed Colonel-General von Weichs, commanding Army Group "B", of the way he thought things were going and Weichs passed this on, together with his own appreciation of the situation, to O.K.H. Here General Zeitzler was sufficiently impressed to propose to Hitler that the attack on Stalingrad should be abandoned and the German 6th Army brought back into the great loop of the Don, whilst the 4th *Panzerarmee* blocked the Stalingrad–Novorossiysk railway opposite Kotel'nikovo.

Hitler's arbitrary solution

Hitler, however, came out with another solution. This was recorded in the O.K.W. diary, then being kept by the historian Helmuth Creiner. The entry for October 26 reads: "The Führer again expresses his concern over a large Soviet attack, perhaps a winter offensive starting in the sector held by our allied armies on the Don and aimed at Rostov. This concern is based on strong troop movements observed in the area and on the number of bridges the Russians have thrown over the river. The Führer orders each of the three allied armies to be stiffened with fighting divisions from the Luftwaffe. This will allow a number of divisions to be withdrawn from the front and, together with other units to be sent to the area, these will build up a reserve behind our allied armies."

This text, the authenticity of which is beyond doubt, is interesting from more than one point of view. First of all it shows that, contrary to what Marshal Eremenko says in his pamphlet against the German generals, O.K.H.'s new Chief-of-Staff had adopted the conclusions reached by Paulus and Weichs and had brought them to the knowledge of the Führer. Especially, however, it shows Hitler's favoured form of reasoning: he discards the approved method which, piecing together information received, consists in asking: "what are the possibilities for the enemy?" to ask the questions such as one might hear at a café-table discussion: "wherein lies the enemy's greatest advantage?" or again: "what would I have done if I had been Stalin?" Now an attack towards Rostov was markedly more advantageous to the Russians than the pincer movement adopted by *Stavka* since, when it had reached its objective, it would have meant the destruction not only of five of Weichs' seven armies, but also of the whole of Army Group "A" right down in the Caucasus. If Stalin had been Hitler he might have adopted this risky solution, but he was not and went for prudence.

Belated decision

The Rostov hypothesis, however, meant that the Italian 8th Army had to be strengthened. This would take the first brunt of any attack in this direction. It was reinforced by the XLVIII Panzer Corps under its recently-appointed commander, Lieutenant-General F. Heim. A few days later Hitler, no doubt on the receipt of further information, seems to have been converted as a very last extreme to Zeitzler's view. It is a fact that on November 16, that is on D-day minus three, XLVIII Panzer Corps received the order to move from Boguchar to Perelazovskiy in the area behind the Rumanian 3rd Army. These two places are 110 miles apart. Too late! We must therefore conclude that, if we accept Marshal Eremenko's view that "Hitler's command" was caught out by the event, this really meant only the Hitler-Keitel-Jodl trinity.

"How many divisions has the Pope?" Everyone knows this question, put by

Stalin to one of his western visitors. But if, 30 years after the event, we ask the authors of Volume III of the *Great Patriotic War* how many divisions Stalin threw into the Stalingrad counter-offensive on the dates indicated, we have to state that no precise reply is obtainable, whereas we know down to regimental level the order of battle of Army Group "B" for November 15, 1942. On that day,

in his headquarters at Star'obel'sk Colonel-General von Weichs held a front from Elista in the Kalmuk Steppe to Kursk, a distance of 710 miles, with 80 divisions, four of which were for the protection of his rear areas, the other 76 being fighting units. The latter were divided into types and nationalities as follows:

	Infantry	Cavalry	Motorised	Armoured	Total
German	31	–	4	5	40
Italian	6*	1	2	–	9
Rumanian	13	4	–	1	18
Hungarian	8	–	–	1	9
Total	58	5	6	7	76

*including 3 Alpine divisions

The fact remains, it is true, that on November 19 and 20 the Soviet pincers bit into only seven German and 15 Rumanian divisions from the 4th *Panzerarmee*, XI Corps (6th Army), XLVIII Panzer Corps, and the Rumanian 3rd and 4th Armies. On the same dates Generals Vatutin, Rokossovsky, and Eremenko were able to engage nine armies, which contained 66 rifle divisions, five tank corps, and a mechanised corps, a comfortable strategic superiority.

The same superiority was apparent in *matériel*. According to the *Great Patriotic*

◁ *"33 anti-tank riflemen", a Russian painting by I. E. Yevstigneyev. It is typical of the style of official painting showing the grim heroism of the Russian defenders.*

△ *An assault group moves in with grenades and sub-machine guns. In October and November Paulus was losing the equivalent of a division every five days, but Hitler had said in a meeting of the Party old guard at the Burgerbräu House on November 9: "I wanted to take the place and we've pulled it off, we've got it really; except for a few enemy positions." And so the fighting had to go on.*

War the following was the picture on the Don battlefield and on the Steppe:

	Russians	Germans and allies	Ratio
Armoured vehicles	894	675	1.3:1
Guns and mortars	13,540	10,300	1.3:1
Aircraft	1,115	1,216	1:1

These figures cannot be accepted, however. According to an entry in the O.K.W. war diary dated November 6, 1942, out of 1,134 Luftwaffe aircraft available over the whole front, *Luftflotte* IV disposed of only 600 which, moreover, had to meet the demands of both Army Group "A" and Army Group "B". As for tanks, the 6th Army's XIV Panzer Corps was reduced to 199 on the day the battle started, as we have seen, and on the day it arrived on the scene XLVIII Panzer Corps only had 84. When we add to these a handful of tanks the 27th Panzer Division and the Hungarian 1st Armoured Division, both of them units in the course of formation, we have scarcely reached the half of the Soviet historian's figure. Moreover, this figure cannot have taken into account the fact that the Panzers included a high proportion of Czech Pzkw 38(t)'s, whose obsolete 37-mm guns had no effect on the thick plating of the T-34's and KV-1's now making up the major part of the Red Army's armoured formations.

Fighting in the skeleton of a city. The Russians had received orders which left no room for misunderstanding: "There is only one road, the road that leads forward. Stalingrad will be saved by you, or be wiped out with you."

△ *While a Degtyarev DP light machine gun covers their moves, a squad of soldiers doubles across a dangerous patch of open ground.*

◁ *Two German soldiers walk through the shattered remains of a factory. Even if they had captured the city there would have been nothing of value for the Germans.*

▷ *The gaunt remains of workers' apartments overshadowed by the thick cloud of smoke from the oil tanks hit by the Luftwaffe on September 27.*

The satellites' part

Even before the start of the battle which was to bring about the final destruction of his army group, Colonel-General von Weichs was not optimistic about the outcome after the adverse reports of his Intelligence units. On the preceding October 10, the Rumanian 3rd Army (General Dumitrescu) had taken up positions between the left flank of the German 6th Army and the right flank of the Italian 8th Army (General Gariboldi). This was in execution of the directive of April 5, which laid down that the Don front should be defended by the satellite powers.

But between the right flank of the Rumanian 3rd Army, which adjoined the left flank of the German 6th Army, and the left flank of the Hungarian 2nd Army (Colonel-General Jany) which adjoined the German 2nd Army, the Don front was some 310 miles long. The three satellite armies which were being asked to defend it had between them some 30 divisions. All of them were somewhat weak in infantry, lacking in mobility and, especially, very badly equipped both qualitatively and quantitatively to meet armour-ed attack. The Rumanian 3rd Army was particularly badly situated as it faced the two bridgeheads at Kletskaya and Serafimovich, where the Russians had held out in the previous summer against all attacks and, without being able to take advantage of the river obstacle, the Rumanian battalions each had an average front of over three miles.

Marshal Antonescu, the Rumanian dictator, had not failed to draw Hitler's attention to the extreme danger of the situation. In particular he had asked Hitler for 5-cm anti-tank guns to replace the earlier 3.7-cm weapons with which the Rumanians were equipped and which were recognised as completely obsolete. The Führer had promised to supply these without delay, but his promise remained empty words and a catastrophe became inevitable. Army Group "B" was thus in position of "pre-rupture".

The position was further blackened by the fact that the strategic reserves available to Weichs consisted of only four divisions, two German infantry divisions and the two armoured divisions of the XLVIII Panzer Corps. One of these two, however, the Rumanian 1st Armoured Division (Radu) had never been in action and both were under strength.

▽ *One German soldier who did reach the Volga. It was the German's failure to squeeze out the Russian salients over the river to the north of the city that left them as jumping-off points for a Soviet counter-offensive. Stalingrad had acted as a magnet drawing in the best of the German forces and the attention of the staff and officers of the 6th Army.*

CHAPTER 73

STALINGRAD: The Trap Closes

The operation, under Zhukov's overall command, had been baptised "Uranus" in Moscow and was launched in two phases.

At 0730 hours on November 19, after a general rocket barrage from *Katyushas*, the artillery of the South-West and the Don Fronts opened up on the German-Rumanian positions with about 90 guns per mile of front. According to the Russians, the density of this concentration was made less effective because of thick fog. Be that as it may, the entire telephone network of the Rumanian 3rd Army was put out of action as the wires were cut by the shelling. The fog also helped the surprise effect. At 0848 the Soviet barrage moved forward, and infantry and tanks flung themselves into the assault.

On the South-West Front, the 5th Tank Army (Lieutenant-General P. L. Romanenko) had as its task the annihilation of the Rumanian defence facing the Serafimovich bridgehead, but it met such resistance that its commander had to use up in the breakthrough some of the tanks he had planned to hold back for exploitation of the breach. But then the defence collapsed. At nightfall, two Soviet tank corps, protected on their flanks by corps of cavalry, broke through the breach and poured into the enemy's rear, causing fearful panic.

Further to the east, the Soviet 21st Army broke out of the Kletskaya bridgehead on a front of nearly nine miles. Under the command of Major-General I. M. Chistyakov, it also had to use its armoured forces to overcome the resistance of the Rumanians. By the end of the day it had had the same success as the 5th Tank Army. The Rumanian V Armoured Corps (General M. Lascar), which was holding out between Kletskaya and Serafimovich, saw that it was doomed to encirclement.

On the Don Front, the Soviet 65th Army (Lieutenant-General P. I. Batov), attacking from the Kletskaya bridgehead towards Vertyachiy, where the Germans had bridged the Don, was caught at a disadvantage in deep ravines. It also ran up against the XI Corps, which formed the left flank of the 6th Army, and was counterattacked furiously by the 14th Panzer Division. It was therefore able to make only modest advances. The 24th Army

△ *A knocked-out Soviet medium anti-aircraft gun and tractor in the autumn mist. At the beginning of the attack on the city the Luftwaffe had total air superiority, and even added scrap iron to more lethal payloads dropped on Chuikov's men. But with the onset of autumn their temporary airfields became mud-bound, and maintenance and loading a gruelling task for the ground crews.*

Major-General I. Galinin), which had been ordered to advance along the left flank of the Don, was similarly held up. The 66th Army (Lieutenant-General A. S. Zhadov) was to make a diversion in the Don-Volga isthmus, stubbornly defended by the VIII Corps (General W. Heitz).

On the Axis side, the XLVIII Panzer Corps, on stand-by since dawn, rumbled off at 0930 hours towards Kletskaya, where it was thought that the main Russian effort was being made, with orders to engage it without worrying about the flanks. Towards 1100 hours, in the light of new information, General Heim was ordered to drive towards Sera-movich—a switch from north-east to north-west. In the fog this counter-order produced confusion, contact was lost, and both the 22nd Panzer Division (Major-General Rodt) and the Rumanian 1st Armoured Division ran blindly into the Soviet 5th Tank Army. In the evening Heim was surrounded and his troops were in a very bad way.

On November 20, in accordance with orders received, Colonel-General Eremen-ko launched his offensive on the Stalin-grad Front from a line Krasnoarmeysk—Lake Sarpa—Lake Tsatsa with his 64th,

57th, and 51st Armies under the command respectively of Major-Generals M. S. Shumilov, F. I. Tolbukhin and N. I. Trufanov. To exploit the expected break-through, Eremenko had put the XIII Mechanised Corps (Major-General T. I. Tanichikhin) under 57th Army, whilst the 51st Army had been given the IV Mech-anised Corps and the IV Cavalry Corps (Major-Generals V. T. Volsky and T. T. Shapkin). On the other side, all Colonel-General Hoth had left of his former *Panzerarmee* was IV Corps (General E. Jaenecke), but he did have the Rumanian 4th Army, of which General C. A. Con-stantinescu was about to take over the command. He thus had seven infantry divisions (two of which were German), and two Rumanian cavalry divisions. He held in reserve the excellent 29th Motor-ised Division.

Delayed by fog, the attack started at 1000 hours, but by early afternoon the breakthrough had come in the sector of the Rumanian VI Corps whose 1st, 2nd, and 18th Divisions were virtually wiped out. The 29th Motorised Division tried to restore the situation and scored some early victories. But as the only unit capable of counter-attacking amidst the general rout, it soon had to abandon the positions it had won for fear of being surrounded. Eremenko was not long in letting loose his cavalry and mechanised units, and on the following day, at 1030 hours, IV Cavalry Corps galloped into the village of Abganerovo, a station on the Stalingrad–Novorossiysk railway line. A few minutes later Nikita Khrus-chev was on the scene, bringing con-gratulations and encouragement.

In the great sweep of the Don on this same November 20, Vatutin and Rokos-sovsky energetically exploited their suc-cesses of the day before. The former used his 5th Tank Army and the latter his IV Tank Corps (Major-General A. G. Krav-chenko) and his III Guards Corps (Major-General I. A. Pliev). Meanwhile the 21st Army completed the encirclement of the Rumanian V Corps, which then turned south and fought with some tenacity.

But how could it face an attack by some 900 tanks and two cavalry corps? At dawn on November 20, at Perelazovskiy, the staff of the Rumanian II Corps was so taken by surprise that when the patrols of the XXVI Tank Corps (Major-General A. G. Rodin) reached their headquarters they found tables laden with maps and docu-ments, cupboards open, keys in the locks of

△ *General Rokossovsky, commander of the Don Front, whose troops struck on November 19. A day later the Stalingrad Front under General Eremenko struck from the south of the city. The preparations for the counter-offensive had been a feat of outstanding organisation and secrecy. With the South-West Front under Vatutin, the Russians had about parity of men, and a slight superiority of weapons—but their men were fresh and their weapons were new, and their morale was very high.*

◁△ *Soviet tank riding troops dismount and move into attack. This tank/infantry team allowed each arm to give mutual support in attack, but was expensive in casualties.*

◁▽ *An anti-tank rifleman with his number two waits in the foreground as infantry move into assault. They are well spaced to provide no easy target—the days of the bunched, mass assaults of 1941 are over.*

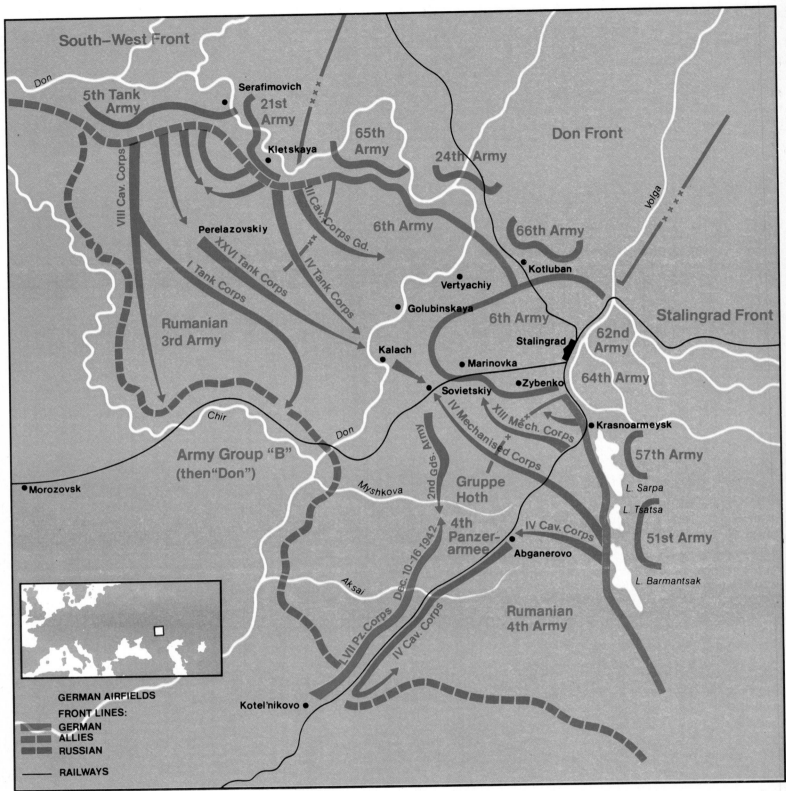

△ *The pincers close. The attacks had been directed at the weak links in the Axis forces and preceded by a massive artillery and mortar barrage which cut communications and stunned the defenders. Then out of the mist came the tanks and infantry.*

chests, teleprinters still connected, and officers' caps still hanging on their pegs. XLVIII Panzer Corps, as a result of a breakdown in radio communications, was out of touch with the Rumanian 1st Armoured Division, but managed to break out of the encirclement. In the evening of November 20 it would have obeyed Weichs' order to retreat had it not had, through a *Führerbefehl*, the overriding order to extricate the Rumanian V Corps. This was an impossible task, and

once again XLVIII Corps was surrounded. Yet it finally managed to reach the German lines, though at the cost of its 22nd Panzer Division, which was reduced virtually to scrap.

The day of November 22 had not yet dawned before destiny had given her verdict. The night before, the Soviet XXVI Tank Corps, forming General Romanenko's left-hand column, was within striking distance of Kalach after covering over 62 miles in three days. The disorder had to be exploited at once and so General Rodin decided to take the bridge over the Don by surprise. He put under the command of Colonel Philippov of the 14th Motorised Brigade a detachment of two infantry companies. They were to advance behind five captured and restored German tanks each carrying 12 men armed with sub-machine guns. Rumbling forward with all their lights on, as the Germans did, Philippov's detachment overwhelmed the bridge guard then drove off the German counter-attacks. The defence was further confused by the shooting-match going on at the same time between the tanks of the 6th Army and those of the Soviets.

Meanwhile Eremenko had eagerly exploited his victory of November 20. Driving his IV Cavalry Corps along the railway from Kuban', he moved his IV Mechanised Corps north-west until at 1030 hours on November 23 it linked up with the IV Tank Corps from the Don Front in the village of Sovetskiy some 18–19 miles south east of Kalach. On the following day Khruschev, whose every movement is recorded in the *Great Patriotic War* in detail, came in person to congratulate Generals Volsky and Kravchenko and to enquire about the needs of the troops. This same day (November 24) saw the end of all Rumanian resistance in the Don pockets. The previous evening General Lascar, who had just been awarded the Iron Cross with Oak Leaves by Hitler, had had to surrender through lack of ammunition. On the 24th General Stenesco did the same and 33,000 Rumanians took the road to captivity.

Hitler determines 6th Army's fate

Events of November 19 found Hitler at Berchtesgaden, whereas O.K.W. was in Salzburg and O.K.H. had for some weeks now been in East Prussia. The Führer's only contacts for three days were by telephone with Zeitzler, and his first reaction was to give command of Army Group "A" to Colonel-General von Kleist, which brought in its train the nomination to the command of the 1st *Panzerarmee* to General von Mackensen, the son of the famous Field-Marshal of World War I. On November 22, however, Hitler decided to go back to Rastenburg. He had already decided the fate of the 6th Army. When

the news reached him that afternoon that it was encircled between the Don and the Volga he ordered, over the heads of Colonel-General von Weichs and General Zeitzler: "The 6th Army will take up a hedgehog position and await help from outside."

A Soviet rocket exploding in Colonel-General Paulus's headquarters could not have had a more staggering effect on the mind of the commander of the 6th Army than this *Führerbefehl*, revealing as it did its author's complete misunderstanding of the tragedy which he was at that moment living. He had just had to evacuate in haste his headquarters at Golubinskaya in the loop of the Don. After consulting four of his five corps commanders he appealed to the Führer in the evening of November 23 on the grounds that he was "better informed".

"Since receipt of your telegram of evening of November 22 events have developed very quickly here. Enemy has not yet succeeded in closing the gap to west and south-west. But his preparations for attack are becoming evident.

▽ *T-34's on the move. The Russians were worried that the 6th Army might decide to break out during the opening moves of the counter-offensive, since the perimeter was neither deep nor secure. They had not allowed for Hitler's reluctance to give up territory he had captured.*

"Our ammunition and petrol supplies are running out. Several batteries and anti-tank units have none left. Supplies not expected to reach them in time.

"Army heading for disaster if it does not succeed, within very short time, in pulling together all its strength to deal knockout blow against enemy now assailing it in south and west.

"For this it is essential to withdraw all our divisions from Stalingrad and northern front. Inevitable consequence will be

that army must be able to drive through in south-west, neither north nor east fronts being tenable after this withdrawal . . .''

At Star'obel'sk Colonel-General von Weichs was still linked to the 6th Army by a telephone line which had escaped the attention of the Russians. When he was told of Paulus's intentions, he vigorously supported them in a message to O.K.H.

"Fully conscious of the unusual seriousness and implication of the decision to be taken,'' he sent over the teleprinter, "it is my duty to advise you that I consider that the withdrawal of the 6th Army as suggested by General Paulus is necessary." He based his opinion both on the impossibility of supplying by air an army of 22 divisions and on the fact that the offensive needed to liberate the 6th Army could not possibly start before December 10 at the earliest. On the other hand, the fighting strength of the 6th Army seemed indispensable to him when it came to rebuilding a front and organising a counter-offensive. This strength had to be regained at all cost. With the help of this brief, which he energetically defended, Zeitzler did so well that at 0200 hours on November 24 he was able to assure the chief-of-staff of Army Group "B" that as soon as he awoke Hitler would sign the withdrawal order asked for by Paulus and recommended by Weichs.

The hours passed. But, instead of the expected confirmation, the radio at Star'-obel'sk received a new *Führerbefehl* aim-ed directly at the 6th Army: "The 6th Army is temporarily surrounded by Russian forces. My intention is to concentrate it in the area north of Stalingrad – Kotluban – Hill 137 – Hill 135 – Marinovka – Zylenko – south of Stalingrad. The Army must be persuaded that I shall do all in my power to supply it adequately and to disengage it when the time is convenient. I know the valiant 6th Army and its Commander-in-Chief and that every man will do his duty.

Signed: Adolf Hitler.''

Göring's responsibility

Shaken by the forceful argument of General Zeitzler, the Führer had been restored to vigour by the exuberant assurances of *Reichsmarschall* Hermann Göring. These were received in silence by Colonel-General Hans Jeschonnek but had the support of Field-Marshal Keitel

Soldiers in the snow. In the second year of the war in the East the Germans had special winter clothing, but as a result of transport and administrative problems it had not reached the 6th Army.
◁ ◁ ◁ *With an L.M.G. at point, and tank support, a group of soldiers prepares to assault a farm house.*
◁ △ *An officer briefs his N.C.O. Both men have only greatcoats and gloves as extra clothing.*
△ *Two ski troops in snow suits on the Terek front in the Caucasus.*

Soviet soldiers clown with a pair of German felt boots. Like those made from plaited straw they were intended to be worn by sentries, but were very impractical compared with those seen on the Russian soldiers.

Sub-machine gunners in position by ruined industrial plant. The weapons which won the battle of Stalingrad were made in the factories that had been so ruthlessly evacuated beyond the Urals at the beginning of the war. It was only later that the Russians would benefit from Lend-Lease trucks and rations in their pursuit of the Germans.

and Colonel-General Jodl. The 6th Army reckoned that it needed 700 tons of supplies a day. This meant the necessary food, animal fodder, petrol, and ammunition to keep going, albeit at a reduced rate, 250,000 men, 8,000 horses, 1,800 guns, and 10,000 vehicles. With a carelessness that can only be called criminal, Göring undertook to assure them of 500 tons a day. He based this on the successful supply of the far smaller pockets at Kholm and Dem'yansk where, for five months from January 1942, 100,000 Germans had held out thanks to supplies from the air. But he was forgetting that:

1. the transport squadrons of the Luftwaffe were no better equipped in November 1942 than they had been the preceding winter;
2. the pocket whose maintenance he was guaranteeing would be 125–250 miles away, or three times the distance of Kholm and Dem'yansk from their supply airfields;
3. the Soviet Air Force, almost non-existent in the first quarter of 1942, had been considerably reinforced since then, particularly in fighters;
4. it would take time to assemble personnel and *matériel* on the bases to be used for this operation; and
5. with the onset of winter, the weather would deteriorate very rapidly.

Indeed, as Colonel-General von Richthofen, the man on the spot, had predicted from the outset, the supplying of the 6th Army by air was a complete and disastrous failure. In actual fact, from December 1 to 12 deliveries to the Stalingrad pocket amounted to an average of 97.3 tons of petrol and ammunition a day. From December 13 to 31 this increased by some 40 tons, then fell again as a consequence of the progressive deterioration of the strategic position and the weather. The average over the whole 70 days of the airlift was 91.16 tons a day, so that Göring's shortfall may be reckoned at 81 per cent. The loss of 488 planes, including 266 Junkers Ju 52's and 1,000 aircrew must also be included on the debit side. On the credit side, 25,000 sick and wounded were evacuated.

In the Stalingrad pocket, to which Paulus had transferred his headquarters, the *Führerbefehl* of November 23 had been the object of bitter argument at the highest level. General von Seydlitz-Kurzbach held that it should be ignored as Hitler did not know the realities of the situation, and that a breakout should be attempted along the line of the railway to Kuban'. Major-General Arthur Schmidt, chief-of-staff of the 6th Army, held the opposite view, both out of respect for orders and because he reckoned that the movement advised by the commander of LI Corps would end in catastrophe compounded by a complete breakdown of discipline. Paulus, though feeling little conviction, decided that his chief-of-staff was right. The German 6th Army thus dug itself into

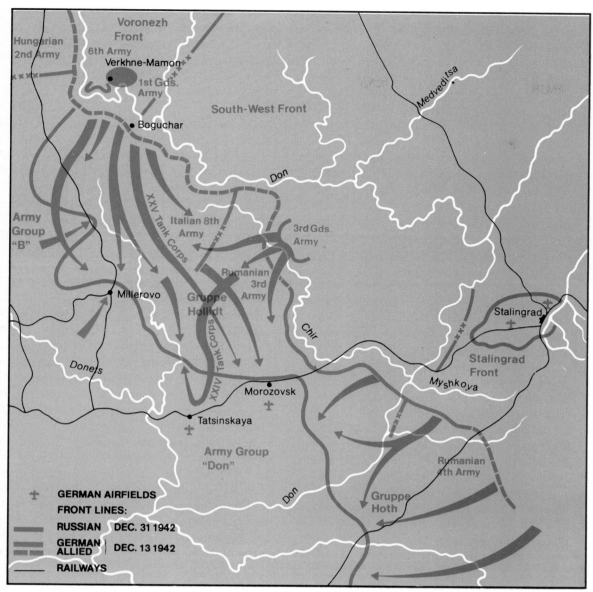

△ An agonised Hitler, in his hand a paper bearing war bulletins, begs for a re-examination of the toothache of the Eastern Front in this Russian cartoon.
◁ No less important than the breakthrough at Stalingrad was the follow-up. The Russians had to put as much territory between the 6th Army and the main German forces as possible. Even so, had the 6th Army attempted a break out during the relief operations mounted in December, there is a chance that a large number of fit men could have escaped.

a pocket measuring some 37 miles between Stalingrad and its western perimeter and 25 miles from north to south. The day after the breakthrough at Lake Tsatsa, IV Corps had come under 6th Army command, though XI Corps, as it retreated across the Don after the surprise attack at Kalach, had taken with it the Rumanian 1st Cavalry Division. Paulus thus commanded five corps, in all 15 infantry divisions, three motorised divisions, three Panzer divisions, and one division of cavalry. These totalled some 278,000 men including the units left outside the pocket.

Manstein's new task

Hitler entrusted the mission of freeing the beleaguered troops in Stalingrad to Field-Marshal Erich von Manstein.

A few days after his victory at Sevasto-pol', the new Field-Marshal, with four divisions of his 11th Army and the great guns which had demolished the Soviets' emplacements, was transferred to Army Group "North" for, in spite of Halder's objections, Hitler had decided to seize Leningrad without waiting for a solution on the Stalingrad front. This offensive, called "Nordlicht", never got started, as the Russians moved first and the 11th Army found itself from August 27 to October 2 using up its strength to bolster up a weakened 18th Army, which had given way, and then having to iron out the salients knocked into the front.

On November 21, when he was in Vitebsk, Manstein received the order to take over forthwith the command of a new army group, Army Group "Don", which would contain the 6th Army, *Gruppen* Hoth and Hollidt, and Rumanian 3rd Army. Its task was defined as follows: "To arrest the enemy's attacks and to regain the ground lost since the beginning of his offensive."

On the 24th he was at the headquarters of Army Group "B", now reduced to the Italian 8th Army, the Hungarian 2nd Army, and the German 2nd Army. Colonel-General von Weichs informed him of the state in which he would find the units allotted to him. Now cut off, the German 6th Army had lost all freedom of movement. Along the line Stalingrad – Novorossiysk, *Gruppe* Hoth was, if the phrase may be permitted, no more than a strategic expression. Having lost its IV Corps and its 16th Motorised Division, immobilised on the Kalmuk Steppe by the express order of Hitler, the 4th *Panzerarmee* was reduced to a handful of Rumanian divisions which had escaped the *débâcle* of November 20. In the great loop of the Don, General Hollidt somehow improvised a defensive line behind the Chir so as to deny to the enemy the defence of the main river.

On November 26 Field-Marshal von Manstein set up his headquarters at Novocherkassk. On the 27th, 78 trains from France arrived in Kotel'nikovo station, 100 miles south-west of Stalingrad, bringing in the first units of the 6th Panzer Division (Major-General E. Raus). These were greeted by artillery fire and began their career on the Eastern Front by driving off the Soviet IV Cavalry Corps. This included a brigade of troops mounted on camels and recruited in Central Asia. Naturally enough, it was virtually wiped out.

Yet it was not before December 10 that the 4th *Panzerarmee*, part of *Gruppe* Hoth, was able to go over to the offensive. It was in fact reduced to nothing more than LVII Panzer Corps (General F. Kirchner), as the Rumanian VI and VII Corps could not be relied on. The 6th Panzer Division was soon up to its full strength with 160 tanks, a battalion of half-tracks, and 42 self-propelled guns. Not so the 23rd Panzer Division (Lieutenant-General von Boineburg-Lengsfeld) hurriedly brought up from the Caucasus, which went into action with only 20 tanks. These figures are important in view of the claims of Soviet historians that Manstein went into action in what they pompously call his "counter-offensive" with 460 armoured vehicles.

On December 12–13, LVII Panzer Corps nevertheless forced a crossing of the Aksai in spite of resistance from the Russian 51st Army of the Stalingrad Front. The valiant Eremenko thought this serious enough to appeal to Supreme Headquarters. "I reported it to J. V. Stalin," he wrote. "Alarmed by this information he sent a message 'Hold out. We will send you reserves immediately.' And he added 'Supreme Headquarters has finally realised what danger you were in.' The situation was becoming very serious: the reserves might be too late." This was why he threw in his XIII and IV Mechanised Corps, in spite of their being worn out. They counter-attacked furiously whilst the Germans put in their 17th Panzer Division, which had only 30 tanks, from the Orel front. The Panzer division's commander, Major-General F. von Senger und Etterlin signalled Hoth: "Situation regarding *matériel* very bad." Hoth replied: "Some divisions up front are even worse off. Yours has an excellent reputation. I am counting on you." The attacks started again and on December 15 Eremenko had to sound the alarm a second time. *Stavka* promised him the prompt aid of the 2nd Guards Army (Lieutenant-General R. Ya. Malinovsky). This army did, in fact, succeed in preventing Kirchner from breaking out of the bridgehead he had won on the north bank of the Myshkova. Hoth had thus won 50 miles in eight days and was within 30 miles of his objective. But he had worn out his men. Conscious of his subordinate's difficulties, Manstein planned to bring over the XLVIII Panzer Corps from the north to the south bank of the Don, which would allow him to take up again the

▷ △ *A Heinkel He 111 is readied for a supply trip to Stalingrad. The Luftwaffe normally managed to get winter uniforms, but these men are as inadequately dressed as their comrades below.*
▷ ▽ *A party of soldiers surrenders in a shell-blasted wood. Their captors are well armed and well dressed.*
▽ *A spotter plane circles over a park of abandoned Marder III Panzerjägers.*

advance towards Stalingrad, from which Paulus now said he could not break out through lack of fuel. But things turned out very differently.

Operation "Saturn"

On December 16, the Soviet High Command set in motion Operation "Saturn" intended as a pincer movement by the South-West and the Voronezh Front (Lieutenant-General F. I. Golikov) to wipe out the Rumanian 3rd Army and the Italian 8th Army and open the way to Rostov. Co-ordination of the attack was entrusted to General Zhukov. The artillery preparation at dawn on D-day required the concentration of 5,000 guns and mortars. On the South-West Front the Russian 3rd Guards Army (Lieutenant-General D. D. Lelyushenko) soon overcame the resistance of the Rumanian 7th and 11th Divisions and forced the XVII Corps to abandon its positions. This done, it exploited its success in the rear areas of the Italian 8th Army (General Gariboldi), whose 230,000 men in nine divisions were deployed on a front of 170 miles. And the Don was now frozen hard enough for tanks to cross. Not only that, but the catastrophe of November 19 had forced Hitler to withdraw its "stays" (the 62nd and 294th Divisions). It had only 380 47-mm guns to defend itself against the enemy tanks, but even twice this number would still have been unable to pierce the Russian armour. Finally, the Italians had only 55 tanks, and these were obsolete. So the army which the boastful Mussolini had flung defiantly at the Russians was now the mere shadow of a real force.

General Golikov had massed in the Verkhne Mamon bridgehead the 1st Guards Army (Lieutenant-General V. I. Kuznetsov) and the 6th Army (Lieutenant-General F. M. Kharitonov). Between them they had 15 infantry divisions supported by many tanks, which operated at battalion strength. Opposite them was the Italian II Corps, with the "Cossiera" and the "Ravenna" Divisions. In such conditions of inequality, the breakthrough took only 48 hours and on December 18 no fewer than five armoured corps poured through the breach which Colonel-General von Weichs was striving in vain to close. How could he have done this when his 27th Panzer Division had only 50 tanks?

△ *The civilians, the real victims of the war. After the fall of Stalingrad, the columns of German prisoners were marched off under only light guard. Frequently bands of armed civilians raided the columns, and exhausted Germans who dropped out were never seen again.*

At Novocherkassk the defeat of Army Group "B" forced Manstein not only to countermand the order to XLVIII Panzer Corps to go to the rescue of the LVII, but on December 23 to order Kirchner to pull the valiant 6th Panzer Division back across the Don. This latter was the only complete formation in the forces designated to free Paulus. It therefore meant that the whole enterprise had been abandoned; This was on a day when the temperature was 30 degrees Centigrade below zero and the men's menu was:

Midday: rice and horsemeat.

Evening: 7 ounces of bread, two meatballs (horse) à la Stalingrad, $\frac{3}{4}$ ounce of butter and real coffee.

Extras: 4 ounces of bread, an ounce of boiled sweets, and 4 ounces of chocolate.

Tobacco: one cigar and two cigarettes.

The significance of this was conveyed by Paulus to a young major from *Luft-flotte* IV attached to his staff. His words betray his emotion and despair: "We couldn't even pull in our outposts, as the men were falling down from exhaustion. They have had nothing to eat for four days. What can I reply, I an Army Commander, if a soldier comes up to me and says, 'Please, Colonel-General sir, a little bit of bread'? We have eaten the last horses. Could you ever imagine soldiers falling on a dead horse, cutting off its head, and devouring its brains raw? How can we go on fighting when the men haven't even got winter clothing? Who is the man who said we would be supplied by air?"

Kirchner was now down to his 17th and 23rd Panzer Divisions with less than 60 tanks between them. Could he hold the Myshkova line? It was unlikely now that the enemy had thrown in the 2nd Guards Army with its numerous powerful armoured formations. The order of December 23 was therefore a sentence of death on the German 6th Army. Also the loss of the aerodromes at Tatsinskaya and Morozovk meant that their supplies had to travel an extra 125 miles.

Manstein could not avoid involvement in this disastrous state of affairs. If Vatutin and Golikov got to Rostov, it would not be only the 6th Army which would be wiped out, but the catastrophe would spread to what was left of Army Groups "Don" and "A". We can only conclude that a system of operations is doomed to destruction when it subjects the commanders to such a dilemma.

"In war, a great disaster always pins great guilt on one man" said Napoleon. In obedience to this dictum Hitler had the commander of the XLVIII Panzer Corps, Lieutenant-General Heim, dragged before a court-martial presided over by Göring. He was condemned to death. Secretly imprisoned in the Moabit Gaol in Berlin, he was released without a word of explanation in May 1943 then, the next year, although banished from the army, nominated commander of the fortress at Boulogne.

CHAPTER 74
Tension at the Top

It was Winston Churchill's job, as he was the driving force behind the Western Allies' change of plan, to explain to the Russians the reasons which had led the British and American Governments to give up all intentions of landing in Europe in 1942 and demonstrate the advantage to the coalition as a whole of a successful Anglo-American landing in French North Africa. Nevertheless, on his request, it was decided by President Roosevelt that Averell Harriman would go to Moscow with him and would help in what the British Prime Minister called "a somewhat raw job."

It had to be shown to Stalin that the new plan being submitted to him resulted not from the lone initiative of the British Cabinet and the Imperial General Staff, but from an inter-Allied decision and that the American leaders were in full agreement with it.

When they were in Teheran, Churchill and Harriman had agreed to hand over the running of the trans-Persian railway to the Americans. This railway, linking the Persian Gulf to the Caspian Sea, had been laid by a British firm and had just been opened to traffic. It could only handle three trains a day in each direction, however (from 300 to 350 tons of goods), and war *matériel* destined for the Soviet Union was piling up on the platforms at Bandar-e-Shāhpūr. As the British were

▽ *As German propaganda saw it: Roosevelt and Churchill struggle for control of Africa. Reality was entirely different. The Americans profoundly distrusted the validity of operations in North Africa, but were forced to accept that an invasion of northern France was impracticable in 1942. They therefore accepted the alternative of "Torch".*

unable to remedy this state of affairs by the delivery of sufficient amounts of rolling stock or by providing enough men to run the line, the Americans got the agreement of their Allies to take over from them, and did the job with complete success. This was the first takeover from the United Kingdom by the United States in this part of the world. The post-war period was to see an acceleration of this process when an exhausted Great Britain's sphere of influence in Turkey and Greece was taken over by the United States.

Churchill and Harriman call on Stalin

At 1900 hours on August 12 Winston Churchill, accompanied by the British Ambassador in Moscow and Averell Harriman, were received in the Kremlin by Stalin, flanked by Molotov and Marshal Voroshilov. We have no record at all from Soviet sources of this or subsequent conversations and we are therefore re-stricted to the account left us by the Prime Minister, filled out with the aid of Lord Alanbrooke's notebooks, although the Chief of the Imperial General Staff did not arrive in the Soviet capital until the 13th. According to Churchill's memoirs, his explanations of the abandon-ment of Operation "Sledgehammer" and his promises to put into execution Opera-tion "Round-up" from April 1, 1943 with 48 divisions, 27 of which would be Ameri-can and 21 British, caused Stalin to "look gloomy", "more and more glum", then to "become restless". The argument that Hitler had not risked crossing the Chan-nel when he was at the height of his power and England had only 20,000 trained men, 200 guns, and 50 tanks, did nothing to calm his irritation.

After an interlude during which he spoke of the bombing of Germany, the British Premier then went on to Operation "Torch" which aroused "intense interest" in Stalin. "In September we must win in Egypt," Churchill said, "and in October in North Africa, all the time holding the enemy in Northern France. If we could end the year in possession of North Africa we could threaten the belly of Hitler's

The Second Front

This was the thorniest problem of 1942, and much loved by the cartoonists of both camps.

◁ ◁ *Stalin's impatience for the Allies to open a Second Front in Europe was matched by that of the British people, as can be seen from this Illingworth cartoon from the* Daily Mail. *So far, Britain's continental ventures (Norway, France, Belgium, and Greece), had been crowned with failure. The left-wingers wanted action.*

◁ *Inter-Allied relations were obvious and easy targets for German cartoons such as this* Simplicissimus *jibe at the three Allied beggars knocking at each other's doors. But even if the doors were opened, all that lay behind were the flames of German victory.*

▷ *Italy too had an interest in the Second Front issue, as is apparent from this Marc' Aurelio cartoon of Churchill exploding with "Stalin must be mad to want a Second Front! Isn't he satisfied with the enemy's victories on the First?"*

Europe and this operation should be considered in conjunction with the 1943 operation. That was what we and the Americans had decided to do."

And he adds: "To illustrate my point I had meanwhile drawn a picture of a crocodile and explained to Stalin with the help of this picture how it was our intention to attack the soft belly of the crocodile as we attacked his hard snout. And Stalin, whose interest was now at a high pitch, said, 'May God prosper this undertaking'."

With a startling quickness of mind the Soviet dictator took in the strategic advantages of the conquest of North Africa which, in his opinion, were as follows:

1. it would hit Rommel in the back;
2. it would overawe Spain;
3. it would produce fighting between Frenchmen and Germans in France; and
4. it would expose Italy to the whole brunt of the war.

Churchill then put forward a fifth argument in favour of "Torch", which was more familiar to him as a former First Lord of the Admiralty than to the Georgian Stalin: the reopening of the Mediterranean to Allied shipping would avoid the interminable detour round the Cape. This would also benefit the Russians, in view of the measures agreed between the British and the Americans to develop traffic on the trans-Persian railway.

"Torch", according to Churchill, pleased everyone; so, after four hours of talks, they separated in a more cordial atmosphere. On the morrow, however, there was a moment when they thought they would have to begin all over again.

On August 13, the Anglo-American delegation, now joined by Generals Brooke and Wavell and Air-Marshal Tedder, was received in the Kremlin at 11 o'clock in the evening. This was to hear read out to them by Stalin a memorandum in which, armed with the Anglo-Soviet communiqué of June 12 (announcing the forthcoming opening of a second front in Europe) he expressed in rather offensive terms his regret at the decision taken on this matter by his Anglo-Saxon allies. "Naturally," he pointed out, "the Soviet High Command was planning its summer and winter operations in relation to this

△ *Averell Harriman, sent by Roosevelt to help Churchill in the latter's "somewhat raw job" of informing Stalin that there would be no second front in Europe in the immediate future. Churchill had asked for Harriman in a message of August 5: "Would you be able to let Averell come with me? I feel that things would be easier if we all seemed to be together."*

The Italian *Semovente* 75/18 assault gun

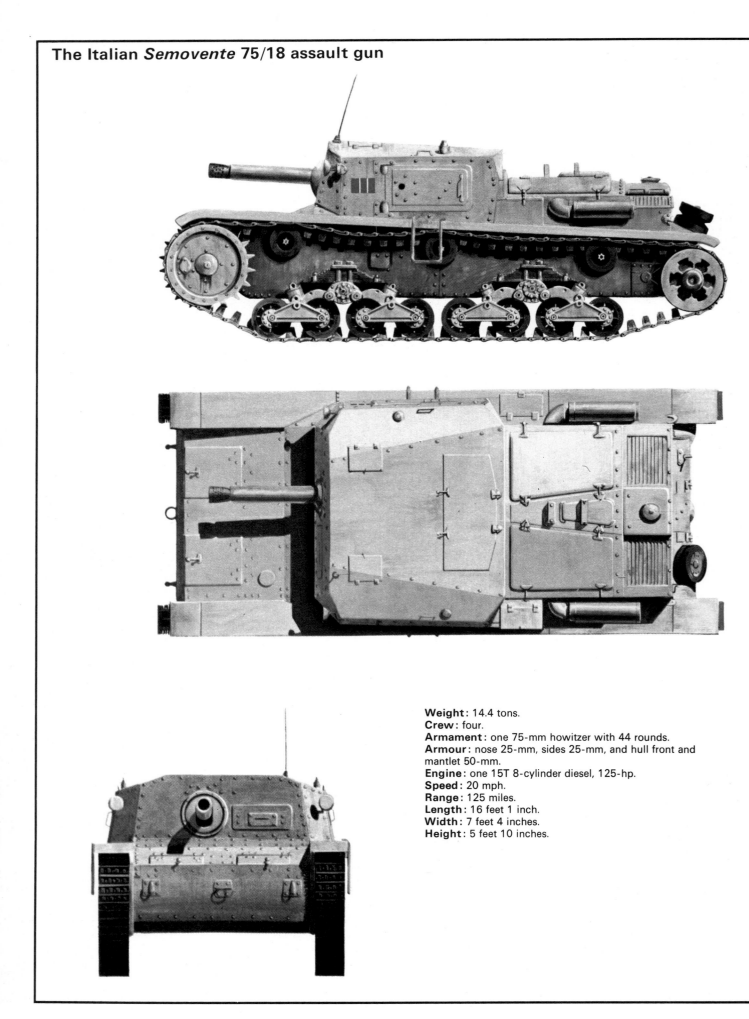

Weight: 14.4 tons.
Crew: four.
Armament: one 75-mm howitzer with 44 rounds.
Armour: nose 25-mm, sides 25-mm, and hull front and mantlet 50-mm.
Engine: one 15T 8-cylinder diesel, 125-hp.
Speed: 20 mph.
Range: 125 miles.
Length: 16 feet 1 inch.
Width: 7 feet 4 inches.
Height: 5 feet 10 inches.

second front. It is easy to grasp that the refusal of the Government of Great Britain to create a Second Front in 1942 in Europe inflicts a mortal blow to the whole of Soviet public opinion; it complicates the situation of the Red Army at the front and prejudices the plans of the Soviet command. I would add that the difficulties arising for the Red Army as a result of the refusal to create a Second Front in 1942 will undoubtedly be detrimental to the military situation of England and all the remaining Allies. It appears to me and my colleagues that the most favourable conditions exist in 1942 for the creation of a Second Front in Europe."

But to his great regret he had to state that he had not been able to convert the British Prime Minister to this view and that the representative of the United States had taken the British side on all these points. He interspersed his reading with questions such as the following, which Brooke noted: "When are you going to start fighting? Are you going to let us do all the work whilst you look on? Are you never going to start fighting? You will find it is not too bad if you once start!"

Indignant at these spiteful imputations, says Brooke, "Winston crashed his fist down on the table and poured forth one of his wonderful spontaneous orations. It began with: 'If it was not for the fighting qualities of the Red Army . . .' Stalin

stood up, sucking on his large bent pipe and, with a broad grin on his face, stopped Winston's interpreter and sent back through his own: 'I don't understand what you're saying, but, by God, I like your sentiment!' " Had he, as Churchill

▽ *A British Light Tank A.A. Mk. I, armed with four 7.92-mm Besa machine guns. Four such vehicles were allocated to the H.Q. of each armoured regiment.*
▽▽ *Valentine tanks in an Egyptian tank depôt.*

experts were about the supplies of Anglo-American war *matériel* to the Soviet Union, the defence of the Caucasus, which Stalin claimed was assured by 25 divisions, and the eventual transfer to that area of a number of British bomber squadrons.

In the morning of August 16, after a long evening in Stalin's villa in the company of Molotov, who "could drink", the Prime Minister flew off to Cairo. He was returning from this first encounter with the Soviet dictator on the whole "definitely encouraged", as he wrote to Roosevelt.

Churchill visits the front

Whilst he was in Cairo, Churchill went to 8th Army headquarters accompanied by General Brooke. Montgomery laid before them, with a skill and an assurance which captivated them, the plan of operations he had drawn up: he would wait for Rommel to attack, knock him out with artillery but without compromising his tanks, then continue with his preparations for an all-out attack which he would let loose only when everything was absolutely ready. In his opinion he would need a week to achieve a breakthrough: then his armour would deal the final blow.

The Chief of the Imperial General Staff managed to get the impetuous Prime Minister to agree to return to London without waiting for Rommel to start his attack. But a few weeks later he had another struggle with him, when Churchill became very displeased at the further time demanded by General Alexander to ready the 8th Army for action, and he wanted to send him a strongly-worded telegram. Once more Brooke poured oil on the troubled waters and managed to pacify Churchill.

But Churchill's arguments were not as unreasonable as Brooke claimed: he was in fact counting on the effect on French public opinion of the defeat of Rommel, expecting that this would give the Allies easier access to the North African ports and, in this respect, September was better than October. On the other hand, the supplying of Malta required the R.A.F. to have control of the aerodromes in Cyrenaica by early November at the latest. Yet any undue haste might cause Montgomery to fail, "Torch" would then be compromised, and Malta virtually lost. As we can see, there was plenty to talk about.

△ *A desert sandstorm. The advent of such a storm meant an immediate halt in all operations, for in such conditions visibility was nil, and it was all that a man could do to protect himself from the ravages of the sand, which percolated everywhere—clothes, body, and equipment.*
▷ *Heartfelt comment from a New Zealand infantryman.*

supposed, been taken to task by his colleagues in the Supreme Soviet for having too easily accepted the fact of "Torch" or, as Brooke thought, had he tried to see just how far he could go with this man whom he was meeting for the first time? We cannot know. In any case, the British Prime Minister could not let pass Stalin's statement that the Anglo-Soviet communiqué of June 12 was a formal engagement by his Government. He reminded him of the aide-mémoire which he had handed to Molotov when the latter came to London and, so that there should be no mistake about it, he confirmed this point of view in a memorandum of August 14:

"3. No promise has been broken by Great Britain or the United States. I refer to paragraph 5 of my aide-mémoire given to Mr. Molotov on June 10 which distinctly says: 'We can therefore give no promise.' This aide-mémoire followed upon lengthy conversations in which the very small chance of such a plan ('Sledgehammer') being adopted was made abundantly clear. Several of these conversations are on record."

Stalin did not refer to the subject again and the rest of the conversations between the two statesmen and their military

RAIDERS OF THE DESERT

The Long Range Desert Group had been formed in 1940 for long range patrol and reconnaissance in the desert. In 1941 the Special Air Service was formed, and from then on the two units operated together in a series of raids behind Rommel's lines. The L.R.D.G. and S.A.S. had a chequered record of spectacular successes and abortive failures, the latter due mainly to bad security and the failure to make full use of 8th Army's intelligence information. This was particularly true of the raids of September 1942 against Benghazi, Barce, Tobruk and Jalo, all costly failures.

1. An S.A.S. patrol—all of them volunteers, used to living rough. Note motley but formidable armament and captured "Jerry-can" containers.

2. A column sets out. Converted Chevrolet trucks were popular but there was no standardisation of equipment. Any suitable vehicle which could be obtained was used.

3. S.A.S. raider mans his twin machine guns.

4. A sketch map of the Axis positions in the Alamein Line, made during a foray deep into enemy territory.

5. A halt in the open desert.

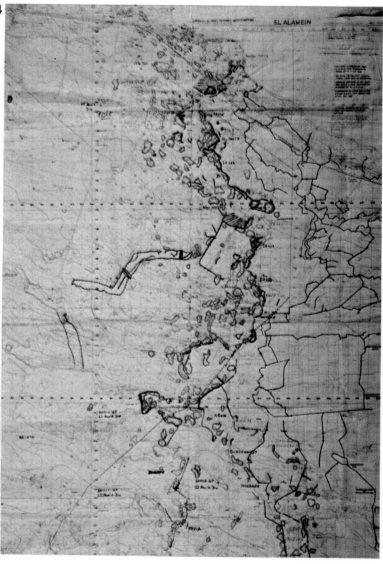

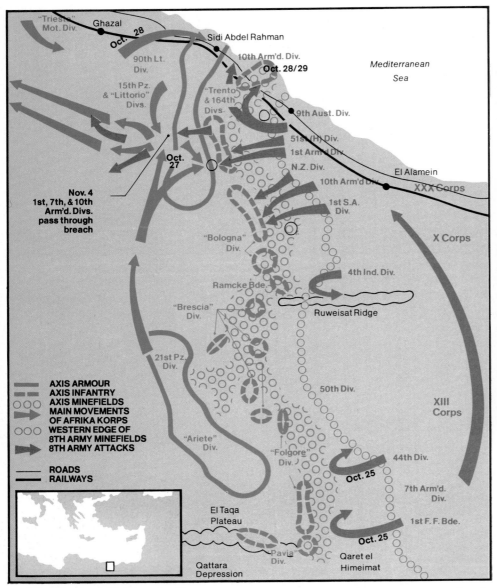

CAMOUFLAGE NETS
Baffle the Hun

△ *The Battle of El Alamein. By careful planning and training, Montgomery was able to outwit Rommel and then crush him with forces superior in numbers, equipment, and preparation.*

△▷ *A moral whose dividends paid off handsomely at Alamein, where Montgomery was able to switch the main weight of his forces from the desert left flank to the coastal right flank unbeknown to Rommel, thanks to meticulous camouflage precautions.*

Previous page: *A 5.5-inch gun/howitzer in action during the short, sharp barrage on October 23 which opened this decisive battle of the North African campaign.*

In his headquarters at Burg el Arab, Lieutenant-General Montgomery still carried on with his preparations for Operation "Lightfoot", as G.H.Q. Cairo called the third British offensive in North Africa. First of all, in the light of experience gained at Alam el Halfa, Montgomery demanded new leaders for XXX Corps and the 7th Armoured Division. For the former he got Lieutenant-General Sir Oliver Leese, formerly commander of the Guards Armoured Division in Britain, and for the latter Major-General A. F. Harding. These were excellent choices, as can be seen from the later careers of these officers: Leese went on to command an army group in Burma and Harding became a Field-Marshal after the war.

One of Montgomery's early decisions was where to make his first attack. So far, Wavell, Rommel, and Auchinleck had all manoeuvred over the desert in order to drive the enemy into the Mediterranean. But by conducting offensive in the north-

ern sector, that is between Ruweisa Ridge and the sea, Montgomery though that there was a good chance that Rom mel would be surprised – provided, o course, that he still believed that Mon gomery himself would stick to the trie and tested tactics used by his predecessor and the Germans. Also, if he moved i from the north, the desert in the sout would play the same part as the sea i offering a complete obstacle in the event a breakthrough. Originally Montgomer had stuck to the tactics laid down by th British and German military doctrine the period: if the enemy's tanks could b knocked out at the beginning, his infantr was at your mercy. He was courageou enough to state that in open ground, give the training of their crews, the Panzer were more manoeuvrable than the Britis tanks and had a good chance of tearin them to pieces. Does this pessimisti statement cause astonishment? It shoul not, since from 1940 onwards the Britis had been constantly changing their tank In two years they had the Matilda, the the Crusader, then the Grant, then th Sherman.

So a change of method was needed an Montgomery has explained this perfectl clearly in his memoirs: "My modified pla now was to hold off, or contain, th enemy armour while we carried out

1020

methodical destruction of the infantry divisions holding the defensive system. These un-armoured divisions would be destroyed by means of a 'crumbling' process, the enemy being attacked from the flank and the rear and cut off from their supplies. These operations would be carefully organised from a series of firm bases and would be within the capabilities of my troops".

Thus Rommel was due for a second surprise. Already deceived about the sector where the 8th Army would make its main thrust, he would also be caught out by his enemy's sudden change of tactics. It could be assumed that he would not remain inactive in face of the danger of seeing his divisions fall apart and then disintegrate. He could be expected to launch counter-attack after counter-attack, but it would only be to find his Panzers deprived of all freedom of movement in the middle of the innumerable minefields protecting the British infantry positions and being fired on by the British armour, waiting steadfastly for them as they had done at Alam el Halfa.

The successful execution of this plan in which nothing was left to chance, required the organisation of a third corps, in addition to XIII and XXX. It would have armoured divisions and its job would be the immediate exploitation of the infantry's advance along the line of the main thrust, then, once a breach was made, to pursue and destroy the enemy. Montgomery got X Corps, under the command of Lieutenant-General Herbert Lumsden. Originally it was to have had the 1st, 8th, and 10th Armoured Divisions, but, to the great chagrin of its commander, Major-General C. H. Gairdner, the 8th had to be disbanded to make up the tank strength of the other two.

British stratagems . . .

The headquarters and communications units played an equally important part in the execution and success of Operation "Bertram". This was the name given by the 8th Army to the deceptions carried out under Major Charles Richardson to convince the enemy that the threat of attack was increasing in the south. To this end the 8th Army used a large number of dummy vehicles, made of rubber and inflated by compressed air. No vehicle left the south for the northern sector with-

out being replaced by a dummy. In the same sector Axis reconnaissance aircraft could watch the laying of a pipe-line, also a dummy, and calculate from the progress of the work that the expected attack would not start before November 1. Finally radio messages from the pseudo-8th Armoured Division made *Panzerarmee* H.Q. think that there was another armoured division between the Qattara Depression and the Ruweisat Ridge.

. . . and camouflage

All this ingenuity would have been of little avail, however, if in the northern sector, where Montgomery was preparing to attack with seven divisions, the 8th Army's camouflage units had not successfully hidden from prying enemy aircraft the thousands of vehicles and enormous storage depôts, and if the secret of Oper-

△ *A Marmon-Herrington armoured car probes into the Axis rear areas at El Alamein as Rommel's forces begin to crumble.*

ation "Lightfoot" had not been jealously guarded. In fact, lower-ranking officers, N.C.O.s, and men were not informed of the offensive until two days before the attack.

Parallel with this enormous effort of organisation, there was an intensive training programme for the troops by Montgomery, a first-class instructor. All this activity explains why, in spite of the Prime Minister's impatience, it was out of the question for the 8th Army to attack before full moon in October, which fell on the 23rd. We may therefore conclude that in once more tempering the ardour of Winston Churchill, General Sir Alan Brooke showed himself to be a truly great servant of his country and a useful artisan of her final victory.

German and Italian deployment

On the other side, Rommel had left Africa and handed over command of the *Panzer-armee* to General Georg Stumme, who had played an important part at the head of the XL Motorised Corps in Greece and then maintained his high reputation in Russia. This new posting relieved him of the disgrace into which he had fallen with the Führer as a consequence of his corps' operations orders falling into the hands of the Russians on the eve of Operation *"Blau"*, Germany's 1942 Russian offensive. He had merely a holding position, however, and was not allowed to take any initiatives, having to content himself with the programme left him by Rommel.

The armoured elements of the *Panzer-armee* had been withdrawn from the front as the force went over to the defensive. This left in contact with the enemy five infantry divisions, one of which was German (the 164th), the "Folgore" Airborne Division, and the Ramcke Brigade. A group composed of the "Ariete" Armoured Division and the 21st Panzer Division held the southern sector, the 15th Panzer Division and the "Littorio" Armoured Division the northern sector. In army reserve, the 90th Light Division and the "Trieste" Motorised Division were deployed in depth along the coastal road. Thus the 164th Division and two battalions of the Ramcke Brigade together with the Italian XXI Corps held the position

continued on Page 1029

◁ ◁ A shell explodes among the front line wire entanglements. But though H.E. shell could destroy this kind of obstacle, mines were left intact, ready for the first unwary foot or track to detonate them. It was here that the Royal Engineers, with their mine detectors, and the mine-clearing "flail" tanks, with their thrashing drum-mounted chains whirling in front of them, played a decisive role in opening corridors for the forces that were to whittle away the Axis infantry.
◁ Classic infantry scene – an Australian officer, armed with a revolver, leads his men forward to the attack, covered by a smoke screen.
◁▽ British infantrymen, bayonets fixed, move forward to the attack. It was upon the Allied infantry forces that the main onus of the Battle of El Alamein fell, contrary to the tactical practice that had become normal in North African operations. Once the Axis infantry had been beaten by that of the Allies, Rommel's armour was left defenceless and was destroyed piecemeal by the superior British armoured formations.

MONTY
The first "Pop general"?

Abrasive, opinionated, at times infuriating to superiors, equals, and subordinates alike, "Monty" was inimitable. The key to his character was supreme confidence and refusal to allow himself to be diverted by worrying over details. Added to all this was a genuine flair for "getting through" to the rank and file, to make them feel that they were being led by a no-nonsense general who knew what he was doing. The sum total was the most colourful British general of World War II, who delivered the goods by winning victories.

Bernard Law Montgomery was born on November 17, 1887, the son of a London vicar. In 1889 his family moved to Tasmania, where his father had been appointed Bishop, to return in 1901. Bernard then spent five years at St. Paul's School before entering Sandhurst in January 1907. He passed out in 1908, joining the Royal Warwickshire Regiment, with which he went to war in 1914 as a platoon commander. Twice wounded on the Western Front, Montgomery was awarded the D.S.O. and ended the war as Chief-of-Staff of the 47th (London) Division.

Montgomery was shocked by the murderous cost of the fighting in World War I, and by the Olympian detachment of the High Command from the fighting troops. These were lessons he never forgot.

He married in 1927, Betty Carver, a widow with two sons. Montgomery and his wife were a devoted couple, and their son David was born in 1928. But the marriage ended in tragedy, with Montgomery's wife dying in 1937 after a long illness. It was a tremendous blow. In his memoirs Montgomery writes "The three outstanding human beings in my life have been my father, my wife, and my son. When my father died in 1932, I little thought that five years later I would be left alone with my son."

In 1939 Montgomery was given command of the 3rd Division and took it to France with Lord Gort's B.E.F. The end of the disastrous Dunkirk campaign saw Montgomery commanding II Corps during the final evacuation. He later commanded V Corps and XII Corps during the "invasion scare" period and was promoted commander of the South-Eastern Army (Kent, Surrey, and Sussex) in December 1941. It was in this capacity that he supervised the Army planning for the raid on Dieppe, carried out against his advice with appalling losses.

In August 1942 Montgomery was informed that he would be commanding 1st Army during "Torch", the scheduled landings in Tunisia—but this plan was dramatically changed when General Gott, who was intended to take over 8th Army in the command shake-up in the Middle East, was killed in Egypt. Gott's replacement was Montgomery.

In taking up his command he was intensely lucky. Auchinleck had fought Rommel to a halt in Egypt and splendid new supplies of superior tanks and guns were already on their way to the Desert. But there were snags. It was clear that Rommel was going to make one last attempt to turn the Alamein line and 8th Army's morale was not good. Montgomery's first battle would be not so much to hold Rommel but to stiffen 8th Army's backbone to defeat the new attack and pass to the offensive for good.

He did this by issuing orders that there would be no further retreat at any cost, by touring the front and showing himself to the men—with the gimmick of a flamboyant selection of cap badges as his identifying mark. Another notable contribution to 8th Army's morale reconstruction was his cracking down on what he called "bellyaching"—pessimistic quibbling by subordinate commanders.

And the first, vital victory at Alam Halfa at the beginning of September 1942 was the well-earned result.

With new heart and the scent of victory, Montgomery and 8th Army now prepared for the decisive breakthrough on the Alamein Line.

1. The "Monty touch"–Australian bush hat and a motley scattering of badges.

2. As a divisional commander with the B.E.F. in France (on right of picture). Montgomery was the first British general to wear serge battledress.

3. Montgomery with his son in 1941, the year he became an army commander.

4. Monty studies his map, wearing his familiar rig–two-badge beret and grey pullover.

5. "I've come here to have a talk with you . . ." Troops press round Montgomery during one of his frequent, informal pep-talks in the field.

6. On an air trip to the Middle East Staff College before the big attack at Alamein.

7. Surveying the battle front from his tank.

8. Touring the front with Churchill during the Prime Minister's visit to the Middle East. "He gave us a masterly exposition of the situation," writes Churchill, "showing that in a few days he had firmly gripped the whole problem." Montgomery, however, was no less subject than his predecessors to pressure from Churchill for a speedy offensive, and he had to be firm. Churchill was disappointed but nevertheless impressed. "Everybody said what a change there was since Montgomery had taken command. I could feel the truth of this with joy and comfort."

9. Monty takes a break for tea with his tank crew.

10. Posing for the cameras in front of a Grant tank. For the coming showdown with Rommel, Montgomery was determined to emulate the way the Afrika Korps fought and keep his armour concentrated.

11. *Montgomery confers with his staff. He insisted that 8th Army must fight as an army, and not as before—"in brigade groups, Jock columns, and with divisions split up into bits and pieces all over the desert."*

12. *Hefting a* kukri *knife during a visit to a Gurkha unit.*

where the enemy attack was expected, while two battalions of paratroopers were stationed with X Corps south of the Ruweisat Ridge.

The time taken to mount Operation "Lightfoot" was naturally not wasted by the Axis forces, which were deployed in depth and considerably strengthened. The units were contained within closed strongpoints protected by more than 445,000 mines, of which 14,000 were anti-personnel ones intended to discourage the enemy's engineers. Under the direction of Colonel Hecker, Rommel's chief of engineering, Italian and German engineers had also contrived booby traps of truly diabolical imagination, using even aeroplane bombs. These defences were naturally covered by machine guns and anti-tank guns. As regards the latter, on October 23, 1942 the D.A.K. had 86 8.8-cm weapons and 95 Russian 7.62-cm guns, of which 30 had been mounted on Czech tank chassis. The British considered these almost as deadly as the famous "88".

It was a hard nut to crack. But between the opposing shores of the Mediterranean, traffic conditions had not improved. Far from it, though Cavallero had thrown in everything he could get hold of. In September 40,465 tons of war *matériel* and 31,061 tons of petrol reached North Africa, 80 per cent of the supplies loaded in Italy. But in October losses rose to 44 per cent and the Axis forces opposing Montgomery got only 12,308 tons of liquid fuel. Cavallero asked Kesselring to put pressure on Malta; he replied by recalling some bomber squadrons from Libya. Although 300 twin-engined German bombers took part in this renewed offensive, it was a total failure and the losses were so heavy that Göring, going over the head of *Comando Supremo* on October 20, ordered it to stop.

"Lightfoot" is launched

At 2140 hours on October 23, 1942, the El Alamein front lit up with a blaze of gunfire over its whole length. Between the sea and Ruweisat Ridge 456 guns opened fire to blast the way open for XXX Corps. In the south XIII Corps had 136 guns.

The attack was a complete surprise: at the time the battle started the commanders of the Italian XXI and X Corps (Generals Navarrini and Nebbia respectively) were on leave in Italy and only got back

to their H.Q.s at the same time as Rommel. This was the curtain-raiser for 12 days of battle fought out between 12 Axis and ten Allied divisions, though these numbers are misleading: Montgomery had the advantage in both men and *matériel*. The following table gives the comparative figures. It is taken from the official Italian account of the battle and was published in 1961 by the Historical Services of the Italian Army:

Strengths of the forces engaged on the El Alamein front on October 23, 1942
(Italian figures in brackets)

	Panzer-armee	8th Army
Infantry battalions	70 (42)	86
Field guns	571 (371)	939
Anti-tank guns	522 (150)	1,506
A.A. guns	1,350 (750)	811
Tanks	497 (259)	1,348
Armoured cars	a few dozen	500

This table does not show that the defenders were short of ammunition and fuel, whereas Montgomery was more than abundantly supplied. Also, the Axis had nothing to compare with Sir Arthur Tedder's 1,200 planes, in particular Air

◁ *German armour waits for the Allied wave to break upon it. Bereft of the infantry support so essential to large scale armoured warfare, Rommel's tanks could not hold the El Alamein position against the imaginative and more numerous Allied tank forces.*

△ *Ready to go. The commander of a British Crusader tank, perched on the turret roof of his vehicle, waits for the command to move off at dawn on October 26. Note the identification marks deleted from the print by the war-time censor. Though the tank was in this, like most North African battles, the final arbiter, it was the infantry artillery that had paved the way for it.*

The German Pzkw III Special medium tank

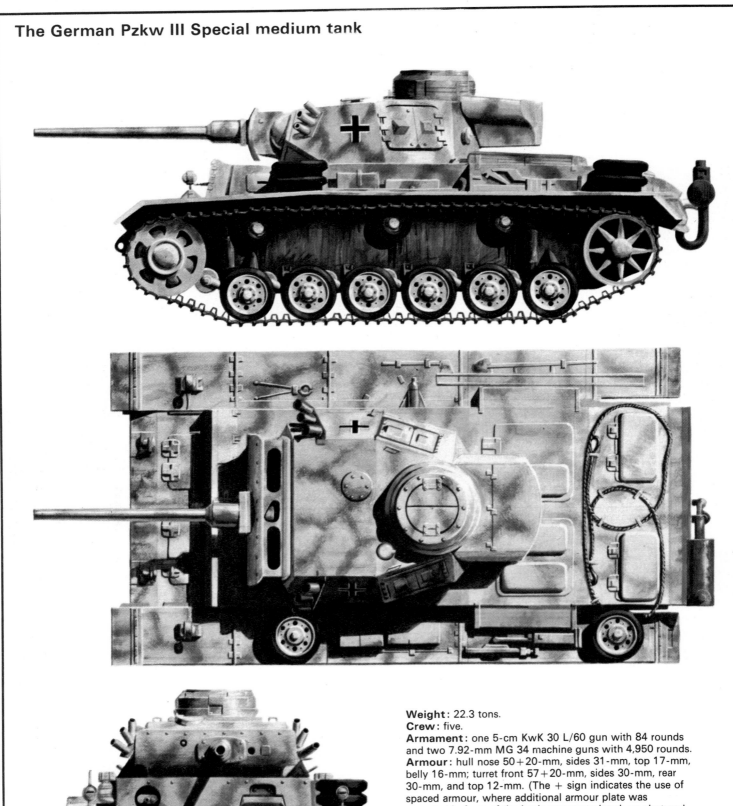

Weight: 22.3 tons.
Crew: five.
Armament: one 5-cm KwK 30 L/60 gun with 84 rounds and two 7.92-mm MG 34 machine guns with 4,950 rounds.
Armour: hull nose 50+20-mm, sides 31-mm, top 17-mm, belly 16-mm; turret front 57+20-mm, sides 30-mm, rear 30-mm, and top 12-mm. (The + sign indicates the use of spaced armour, where additional armour plate was mounted in front of the basic armour to break up shot and prevent shells reaching the main armour.)
Engine: one Maybach HL 120 TRM 12-cylinder V, 300-hp.
Speed: 25 mph.
Range: 110 miles.
Length: 21 feet 4 inches.
Width: 9 feet 10 inches.
Height: 8 feet 4 inches.

Vice-Marshal Coningham's 550 light bombers and fighter-bombers.

The 8th Army's artillery barrage lasted 15 minutes. It effectively silenced the enemy's batteries and damaged his telephone communications and minefields, where many of the aircraft bombs were blown up. At 2200 hours the sappers advanced into no-man's-land, using the first mine-detectors to reach North Africa. Behind the sappers there were a small number of "Scorpion" tanks, special adaptations of ordinary tanks, designed to set off mines with whirling flails attached to a drum in front of the tank.

Behind these followed the infantry, with fixed bayonets.

In the southern sector, XIII Corps (Sir Brian Horrocks), whose rôle was to put on a diversionary attack, had been ordered to hold back its 7th Armoured Division. The advance of its major infantry formations, 44th Division (Major-General I. T. P. Hughes) and 50th Division (Major-General J. S. Nichols) was consequently limited and secured at heavy cost against the determined resistance of the "Pavia" and "Brescia" Divisions and the paratroops of the "Folgore", commanded respectively by Generals Scattaglia, Brunetti, and Frattini. On the left flank, the 1st Fighting French Brigade confirmed its fighting spirit on the Qaret el Himeimat, but had to yield some of the ground it had won. Horrocks' objective had been reached: to prevent the enemy from deploying the "Ariete" Armoured Division (General F. Arena) and the 21st Panzer Division (Major-General von Randow) in support of the rest of the Axis forces in the northern sector.

The Axis infantry crumbles away

In the northern sector, XXX Corps' job was to make an inroad along two "corridors" in the minefields. The right-hand corridor was given to the 9th Australian

△ *A mine detonates beside a truck carrying motorised infantry up towards the British front. It was essential that such infantry assault as soon as the sappers had cleared a corridor through the minefields· and so Montgomery's foresight in concentrating most of his transport in the crucial sectors was of prime importance in the successful outcome of the battle.*

△ *Not even the mighty "88"*
could halt the remorseless
advance of Montgomery's troops.
The doubts of the above gun's
crew to the successful outcome
of the action in which they are
engaged seems to be indicated by
the fact that they have brought
their gun into action on its
carriage rather than on its fixed
mounting.
△ ▷ *A captured British truck, in*
service with the Germans, on
fire as Rommel's front begins to
crumble.
△ ▷ ▷ *A German staff car in*
flames.
▷ *Part of a British column moves*
past the wreckage of a Junkers
Ju 52 transport at Fuka.

Division and the 51st (Highland) Division, newly arrived in North Africa and commanded by Major-General D. N. Wimberley; the left-hand corridor went to the New Zealand Division. None of these divisions reached the objectives marked for them on the map, but their action began the destruction of the enemy infantry, as foreseen by Montgomery. The "Trento" Division (General Masina) was very badly mauled and the 164th Division (Major-General Lungershausen) had two of its battalions virtually wiped out.

But General Montgomery was not satisfied with this, and thought that X Corps and the 1st and 10th Armoured Divisions (Major-Generals R. Briggs and A. H. Gatehouse) had not shown sufficient drive and initiative in pressing close on the heels of the enemy infantry. On the other side, General Stumme, who was roaming the battlefield alone, had a heart attack and fell from his vehicle without his driver noticing it. His death was a considerable blow to the Axis forces and his command was taken over in the evening of the 24th by the commander of the D.A.K., Lieutenant-General Ritter von Thoma.

On October 25 Montgomery ordered XIII Corps to press its attack further and XXX Corps to press forward with tank support and under cover of powerful artillery barrages. He was not a man to be discouraged by the stubbornness of the enemy's resistance, but he never dropped his guard and the Axis armour's counter-attacks ran into a veritable wall of gunfire. The battle thus took on something of the character of a conflict of *matériel*, in which Rommel was going to be in short supply.

Rommel sees his danger

When he got back to his H.Q. in the evening of October 26, Rommel realised exactly how serious the situation was. It had been saved only by the engagement of the 90th Light Division and the armoured group in the northern sector. Major-General von Vaerst's 15th Panzer Division had only 39 tanks left and General Bitossi's "Littorio" Armoured Division only 69. He therefore ordered the 21st Panzer Division to move north of Ruweisat Ridge, but 48 hours later it had lost 58 of the 106 tanks it had had on October 23, and by moving it Rommel allowed Montgomery to hold back the 7th Armoured Division from XIII Corps. In XXX Corps, the 9th Australian Division

struck north-west and trapped the 164th Division against the sea. The 1st South African Division (Major-General D. H. Pienaar) and the 4th Indian Division (Major-General F. I. S. Tuker), which formed Sir Oliver Leese's left flank, made a deep penetration into the positions of the "Bologna" Division (General Gloria). On October 29 Rommel wrote to his wife: "The situation continues very grave. By the time this letter arrives, it will no doubt have been decided whether we can hold on or not. I haven't much hope. At night I lie with my eyes wide open, unable to sleep for the load that is on my shoulders. In the day I am dead tired. What will happen if things go wrong here? That is the thought that torments me day and night. I can see no way out if that happens."

Churchill's impatience

In London, however, Winston Churchill could not contain his impatience and summoned General Brooke to his office the same day. "What," he asked, "was *my* Monty doing now, allowing the battle to peter out? (Monty was always *my* Monty when he was out of favour.) He had done nothing now for the last three days and now he was withdrawing troops from the front. Why had he told us that he would be through in seven days if all he intended to do was to fight a half-hearted battle?"

Montgomery redoubles his efforts

As usual the Chief of the Imperial General Staff was able to placate Churchill and was well seconded in this by Field Marshal Smuts, who enjoyed the Prime Minister's special confidence. Montgomery had, in fact, withdrawn one brigade each from the 44th, 50th (XIII Corps), and 51st (XXX Corps) Divisions and given them to the New Zealand Division which, under Major-General Freyberg, was to be the spearhead of Operation "Supercharge" for the decisive breakthrough. Meanwhile XXX Corps had continued to hammer the enemy and forced Rommel to engage the "Ariete" Armoured Division and the "Trieste" Motorised Division, his last reserves.

"Supercharge" was being followed in London with some anxiety: "During the morning," Montgomery records, "I was visited at my Tactical H.Q. by Alexander and by Casey who was Minister of State in the Middle East. It was fairly clear to me that there had been consternation in Whitehall when I began to draw divisions into reserve on the 27th and 28th October, when I was getting ready for the final blow. Casey had been sent up to find out what was going on; Whitehall thought I was giving up, when in point of fact I was just about to win. I told him all about my plans and that I was certain of success; and de Guingand spoke to him very bluntly and told him to tell Whitehall not to bellyache."

"Supercharge", unleashed on November 2, gave rise to battles of a ferocity unheard of in this theatre. Italian anti-tank guns fired on British tanks at a range of 20 yards and one of General Freyberg's brigades was reported to have lost 75 of the 94 tanks it had started with at zero hour. At the end of the day, and in spite of repeated attacks by the Desert Air Force, what remained of the Axis army had managed to form the semblance of a front,

▽ *British soldiers examine part of the spoils of their victory.*
▷ *A German corpse, covered with flies, lies slumped over the edge of the trench where it fell.*
▷ ▷ *British troops experiment with clothing abandoned by a makeshift Italian front line quartermaster's stores.*
▷ ▽ *Prisoners from Rommel's* Panzerarmee Afrika, *some of the 30,000 prisoners taken by the British. The total bag included nine generals and 10,724 Germans.*

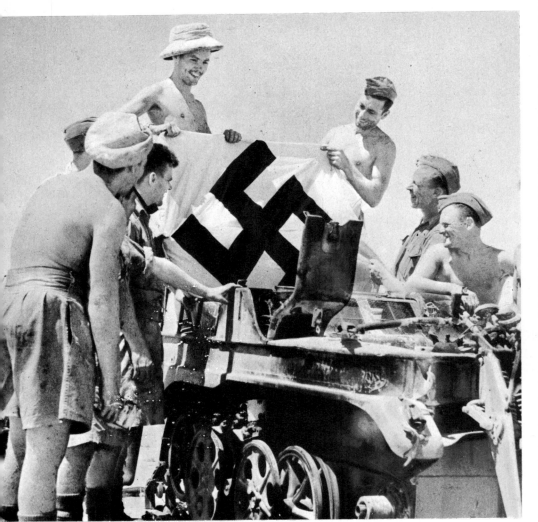

but this was the end. Rommel now had only 187 tanks, 155 of which were Italian and incapable of withstanding the fire of the Shermans. The German tanks were too few to make any considerable contribution.

Hitler orders the *Afrika Korps* to its destruction . . .

Rommel drew his conclusions from the situation and ordered his troops to withdraw. The movement had just begun when, on November 3 at 1330 hours a message from Hitler, a *Führerbefehl*, reached him. It was drawn up in the following terms:

"To Field-Marshal Rommel,

"In the situation in which you find yourself there can be no other thought but to stand fast and throw every gun and every man into the battle. The utmost efforts are being made to help you. Your enemy, despite his superiority, must also be at the end of his strength. It would not be the first time in history that a strong will has triumphed over the bigger battalions. As to your troops, you can show them no other road than that to victory or death."

△ *A Hawker Hurricane IID tankbuster swoops over the desert in pursuit of its prey. The 40-mm cannon of such Hurricanes could rip open German tanks as though with a tin opener.*

. . . and precipitates the British victory at Alamein

As the disciplined soldier that he was, Rommel cancelled his order and made his troops reoccupy their positions. Hence he was defeated on the following day, though, on the report of a special envoy sent to him by plane, Hitler had changed his mind and restored his liberty of action. In the afternoon of November 4 the 8th Army made a breach 15 miles wide in the thread-like front of the enemy in the area of Tell el Aqqaqir. The tanks of X Corps broke through, demolished the "Ariete" Armoured Division in spite of heroic resistance and captured the commander of the D.A.K., General von Thoma, as he leapt out of his blazing vehicle. A few remnants of the D.A.K.'s four divisions escaped from the disaster, together with parts of the "Trieste" Motorised Division and the "Littorio" Armoured Division. The whole of the Italian infantry, however, (the "Trento", "Bologna", "Brescia", and "Pavia" Divisions) were left stranded, as

were the "Folgore" Airborne Division and the headquarters of X Corps. 108,000 troops took part in this battle: the Axis powers lost 25,000 killed and wounded and 30,000 prisoners, including nine generals and 10,724 Germans. A thousand guns and 320 tanks were destroyed or captured by the victors. The Allies lost 13,560 men, of whom 4,610 were killed or missing; most of the missing turned out to be dead. Some tanks were put out of action, 150 irreparably. And so the battle of Alamein ended. Not only had Axis strength in North Africa been broken for ever but so was Rommel's morale, so that not for a moment did he consider making another stand at Halfaya and El Agheila, as *Comando Supremo* ordered. This gave rise to new friction between the Axis partners which was to bear fruit in 1943.

The long retreat starts

El Alamein was over. Rommel now started on his long retreat to Tunis, followed steadily by Montgomery's 8th Army, that was to see the end of Axis power in Africa.

CHAPTER 76
CORAL SEA: the curtain raiser

The question of whether the neutralisation of the American aero-naval forces based on Pearl Harbor should be exploited by a landing on the island of Oahu had been discussed in Tokyo during the detail planning for the December 7 attack. The answer had been "no". Those responsible for Japanese strategy were content with knocking out the main U.S. fleet, thus gaining the time necessary for their forces to overrun South-East Asia. After that they would consider the matter again.

And so, after the capture of Guam and Wake, in the south-eastern Pacific theatre, the Japanese contented themselves with the occupation of the Gilbert Islands, on which they based their major defensive hopes.

The Americans think again

The disaster of December 7 put paid to Operation "Rainbow" for the conquest of the Marshall and the Caroline Islands and the organisation of an American base at Truk. The Pacific Fleet had had an offensive mission; now it was on the defensive, but this was only for the time being and

there was no danger that it would become a passive force. This was the idea which Rear-Admiral Husband E. Kimmel expressed in a note to Navy Secretary Knox on December 11, 1941 when the latter arrived in Pearl Harbor:

"With the losses we have sustained, it is necessary to revise completely our strategy of a Pacific war. The loss of battleships commits us to the strategic defensive until our forces can again be built up. However, a very powerful striking force of carriers, cruisers and destroyers survives. These forces must be operated boldly and vigorously on the tactical offensive in order to retrieve our initial disaster."

In support of this opinion it should be said that on that same day the Pacific Fleet still had in fighting trim the aircraft-carriers *Lexington*, *Saratoga*, and *Enterprise*, 16 cruisers, 44 destroyers, and 16 submarines, some at sea, others in bases at Pearl Harbor and Bremerton (Washington State). Also, when he heard of the Japanese attack, Vice-Admiral Stark, Chief of Naval Operations, ordered the Atlantic Fleet to send *Yorktown*, a carrier of the same class as *Enterprise*, through the Panama Canal to the Pacific—a vital reinforcement.

Memories of the U-boat war and the battle of the Atlantic have always eclipsed the equally vital submarine war fought out in the Pacific. There the outermost parts of Japan's over-inflated empire depended solely upon supply by sea—and the American submarine force took the offensive right from the start. From a slow beginning during the dramatic events of 1941-42, American submarines wreaked havoc on Japan's Pacific sealanes, sinking well over half of her mercantile tonnage. Tactics varied from the "up the kilt shot" (surfacing astern of the victim and torpedoing from there) to the "down the throat shot" (surfacing directly ahead of the victim and torpedoing him head-on).

◁ ◁ *In the control room, scanning the surface through the periscope.*

◁ *The torpedo-room, showing the crew in position for a shoot. The man on the right with the head-set is taking the orders from the control-room.*

▷ △ *and* ▷ *Two "kills"– Japanese merchantmen, sunk by prowling American submarines.*

Nimitz takes over the Pacific Fleet

Scarcely had Kimmel formulated his rather optimistic plan than he was relieved of his command and replaced, on Roosevelt's personal choice, by Rear-Admiral Chester W. Nimitz: "a tow-haired, blue-eyed Texan, of the Naval Academy class of 1905. Tactful and modest, sound in his judgement of men and events, he was to prove a thoroughly fortunate choice." Such is the opinion of E. B. Potter, a professor at the Annapolis Naval Academy, with whom Nimitz later wrote books on naval warfare in World War II.

On December 27 Nimitz took over as Commander-in-Chief Pacific Fleet, or Cincpac, with promotion to Admiral, whilst in Washington Admiral Ernest J. King was appointed head of the U.S. Navy, replacing Vice-Admiral Stark. King thus became Cincus, Commander-in-Chief United States Fleet, and addressed his first order to Cincpac, defining his mission in these terms:

"1) Covering and holding the Hawaii-Midway line and maintaining communications with the west coast.

2) Maintaining communications between the west coast and Australia, chiefly by covering, securing, and holding the Hawaii–Samoa line which should be extended to include Fiji at the earliest practical date."

The execution of this order postulated the setting up of an air-sea front running from Dutch Harbor (Alaska) to Midway, including New Caledonia and hinging on Port Moresby in New Guinea. Nimitz could, of course, call upon all possible facilities in the British and Australian possessions in the Pacific. The French territories had gone over to de Gaulle in the summer of 1940 and in the following year an agreement reached between the Free French leader and the American Government gave the same facilities to the Americans in the case of aggression by the Japanese. The Pacific Fleet's task, therefore, was to engage and repel all enemy forces which attempted to force the front described above. But it was not to be restricted within this perimeter. On the contrary it was, as Admiral King is said to have put it, "to hold what you've got and hit them when you can".

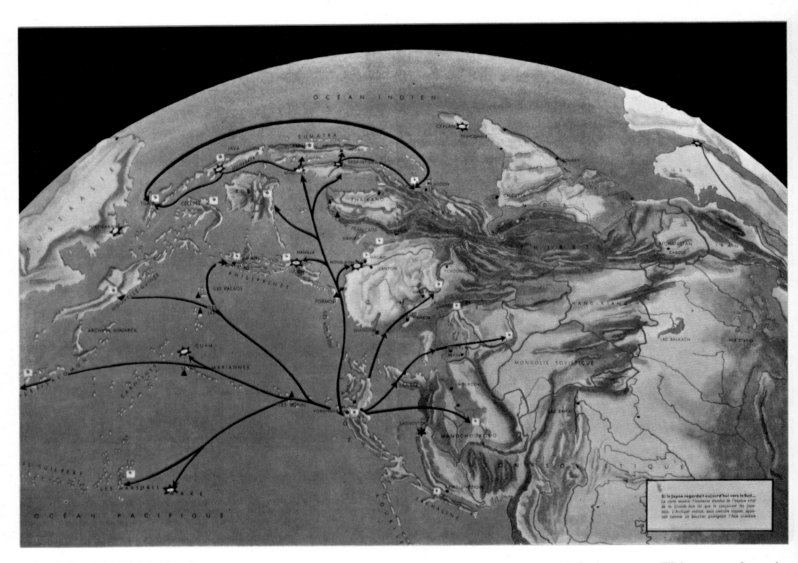

American skirmishes

Admiral Nimitz set about his task as best he could, in spite of the temporary loss of *Saratoga*, damaged by a torpedo on January 11, 1942 and out of service for five months thereafter. On February 1, groups commanded by Rear-Admiral F. J. Fletcher and Vice-Admiral W. F. Halsey, each built round one carrier, "struck", the one in the Gilbert archipelago and the other in the Marshall Islands, to such effect that the Japanese High Command thought it necessary to withdraw the aircraft-carriers *Zuikaku* and *Shokaku* from the fleet then preparing to operate in the Indian Ocean. During another undertaking by Halsey, planes from *Enterprise* bombed Wake Island on February 24, then Marcus Island. The latter was only about 1,100 miles from the Japanese capital.

Annoying though they were, these were only pinpricks, and during this phase of the campaign they were less important than another victory which the Americans

Admiral Chester Nimitz was born in Texas in 1885. He served in World War I as Chief-of-Staff to the Commander of the U.S. Atlantic Submarine Force, and after Pearl Harbor he was made Commander-in-Chief of the Pacific Fleet. His victories at the battles of Coral Sea and Midway crippled the Japanese fleet and assured the safety of the United States from direct naval attack.

won over their enemy. This came about in the shade of an office in Pearl Harbor and was never the subject of any special communiqué. By dint of much patience and perspicacity, the code-breaking unit attached to the Pacific Fleet succeeded in deciphering the Japanese naval code. From then onwards, now that it was known what the enemy was going to do, the enemy was going to be undone, to paraphrase an old proverb.

Aboard the battleship *Nagato,* flying the flag of Admiral Yamamoto in Hiroshima Bay, the Combined Fleet's Chief-of-Staff, Rear-Admiral Ugaki, had been concerned since late January about what the next Japanese naval operations should be. In his opinion, it was important to take advantage immediately of the superiority of the naval and naval air forces enjoyed by Japan to crush the American fleet and seize Hawaii. Among the arguments which seemed to him to point to this conclusion we mention one:

"Time would work against Japan because of the vastly superior natural resources of the United States. Conse-

quently, unless Japan quickly resumed the offensive–the sooner the better–she eventually would become incapable of doing anything more than sitting down and waiting for the American forces to counter-attack. Furthermore, although Japan had steeled herself to endure a prolonged struggle, it would be obviously to her advantage to shorten it if at all possible, and the only hope of so doing lay in offensive action."

But Rear-Admiral Ugaki was unable to convince his Chief of Operations, Captain Kuroshima, who considered that a new attack on Hawaii would no longer have the benefit of surprise. Quite to the contrary, and a Japanese fleet operating in these waters would now have to deal not only with the enemy's naval forces but also with his air force and coastal batteries. In the face of these difficulties Kuroshima opted for an offensive westwards: the destruction of the British fleet in the Indian Ocean, the conquest of Ceylon, and the establishment of contact with the Axis powers. These were the objectives he recommended.

Ceylon is reprieved

Direct co-operation between Japan, Germany, and Italy soon had to be abandoned as the links between the three totalitarian allies were very tenuous. Kuroshima's proposal was nevertheless examined very carefully both by Admiral Yamamoto and at the highest level of the Naval General Staff by Admiral Nagano. This was the state of things in late February when the Army, under the pretext of the Soviet pressure on Manchukuo, refused their co-operation in any attack on Ceylon.

Meanwhile the headquarters of the Combined Fleet had been set up on board the giant battleship *Yamato*. Here Ugaki's arguments against any expectations of assistance seemed still to prevail. So, turned away from Ceylon by the Army's unwillingness, no time was lost in turning the offensive eastwards. Account was taken of the objections against a direct attack on Hawaii and it was therefore

△ ◁ ◁ *"When Japan looks south today"–a drum-beating piece of propaganda from Germany's* Signal *magazine, boasting of the impregnability of Japan's newly-won "southern barrier". But the main weight of the Allied counter-offensive would come not from the south but from the east . . .*

△ ◁ *Battleship* Nagato, *which formed part of Yamamoto's "Sunday Punch" in the Midway plan: the concentrated fire-power of the most powerful battleships in the Combined Fleet.*

△ △ *Rear-Admiral Raymond Ames Spruance, named by Halsey as the ideal man to take over Task Force 16 for the showdown at Midway. It came as somewhat of a surprise, for Spruance was a "battleship admiral"–but it proved an inspired appointment.*

△ *Rear-Admiral Frank Jack Fletcher, veteran of the Coral Sea fight, flew his flag in* Yorktown *at Midway.*

The American aircraft-carrier *Lexington*

Displacement: 36,000 tons.
Armament: twelve 5-inch A.A., twenty 1.1-inch A.A., and twenty-eight .5-inch machine guns, plus up to 90 aircraft.
Armour: 6-inch belt, 1-inch deck, and 3-inch turrets.
Speed: 34 knots.
Length: 888 feet.
Beam: 130 feet.
Draught: 32 feet.
Complement: 3,300.

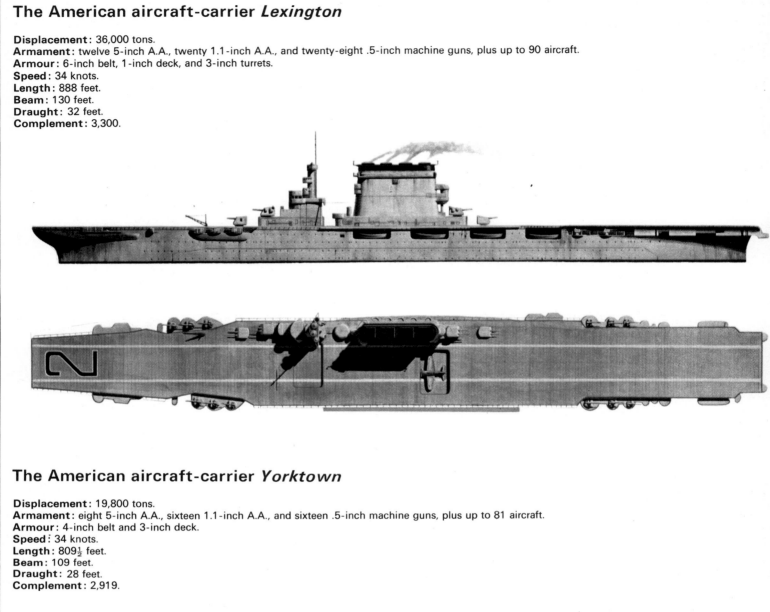

The American aircraft-carrier *Yorktown*

Displacement: 19,800 tons.
Armament: eight 5-inch A.A., sixteen 1.1-inch A.A., and sixteen .5-inch machine guns, plus up to 81 aircraft.
Armour: 4-inch belt and 3-inch deck.
Speed: 34 knots.
Length: $809\frac{1}{2}$ feet.
Beam: 109 feet.
Draught: 28 feet.
Complement: 2,919.

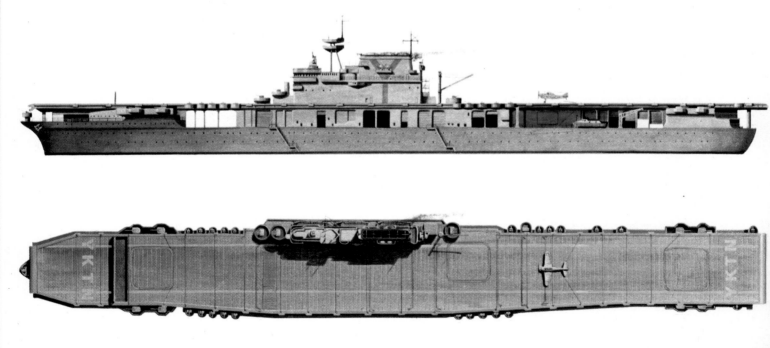

The Japanese aircraft-carrier *Shoho*

Displacement: 11,262 tons.
Armament: eight 5-inch A.A. and fifteen 25-mm A.A. guns, plus 30 aircraft.
Armour: none.
Speed: 28 knots.
Length: 712 feet.
Beam: 59 feet.
Draught: $21\frac{3}{4}$ feet.

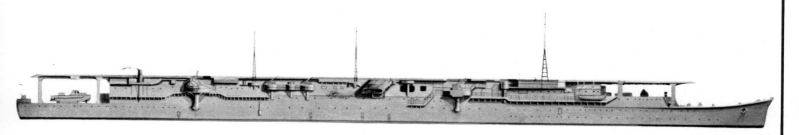

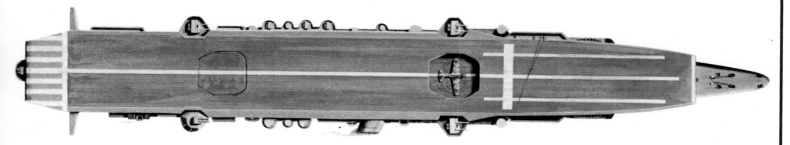

The Japanese aircraft-carrier *Hiryu*

Displacement: 17,300 tons.
Armament: twelve 5-inch A.A. and thirty-seven 25-mm A.A. guns, plus 73 aircraft.
Speed: $34\frac{1}{2}$ knots.
Length: 746 feet.
Beam: $73\frac{1}{4}$ feet.
Draught: $25\frac{1}{3}$ feet.
Complement: 1,101.

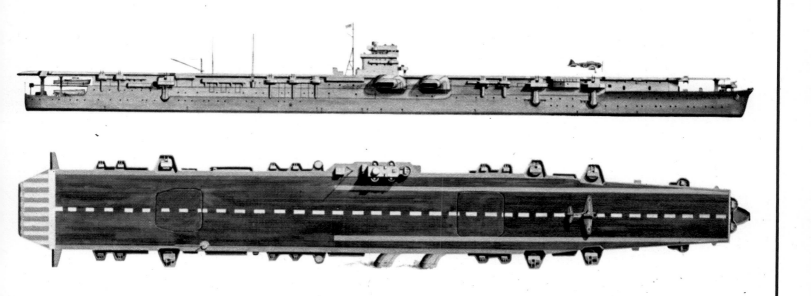

△ △ A B-25 lurches off the deck of the Hornet. These planes coul[] launched but not recovered, and had to continue on to China afte[] their raid on Tokyo.

△ Four of the 62 crewmen who reached China. Their planes were the spearhead of raids that would devastate the Japanese cities.

◁ Bomb damage in Tokyo. The picture shows the Ginza, the city's main thoroughfare.

Section, where Admiral Fukudome was insisting on an attack against Australia. According to Commander Fuchida, whose account of the matter we have drawn on, the "Australian School", as the supporters of an offensive in this area were called, put forward the following arguments:

"Australia, because of its size and strategic location on the Japanese defensive perimeter, would almost certainly become the springboard for an eventual Allied counter-offensive. This counter-offensive, they reasoned, would be spear-headed by air power in order to take full advantage of American industrial capacity to produce planes by mass-production methods, and the effective utilisation of this massive air strength would require the use of land bases in Australia. Consequently, there would be a weak spot in Japan's defensive armour unless Australia were either placed under Japanese control or effectively cut off from the United States."

It is true that the Army had refused the Navy the one division thought necessary to overrun Ceylon, and it had all the more reason to refuse to put ten into an operation such as this. They would content themselves, therefore, with isolating Australia and this would be done by the progressive occupation of New Guinea, the Solomon Islands, New Caledonia, New Hebrides, Fiji, and Samoa.

The "Doolittle Raid"

Admiral Yamamoto did not agree with this line of reasoning. In his opinion the G.H.Q. plan would not give him the great naval battle which he thought so necessary for swift victory. Admiral Nagano supported him, though very much against his better judgement. These differences of opinion continued up to the day of the operation, but on April 18 an event occurred which cut short all discussion: the bombing of Tokyo by a handful of North American B-25 Mitchell twin-engined bombers under the command of Lieutenant-Colonel James H. Doolittle.

These planes weighed 13 tons fully loaded and nothing so heavy had ever taken off from an aircraft-carrier before. Lengthy preparations were therefore necessary. On April 13 the aircraft-carrier *Hornet*, with 16 of these B-25's on board, rendezvoused with Task Force 16, under Halsey, which was to escort her. The plan

decided to mount an operation for the capture of Midway. This objective was far enough away from Oahu to prevent interference by land-based American aircraft; it was also important enough to compel the enemy fleet to fight, and without land-based support this would allow the Japanese battleships and aircraft-carriers to use their as yet undoubted superiority.

Admiral Yamamoto approved the plan submitted to him for the attack on Midway and sent it forward on April 2 for approval by the Naval High Command. But in Tokyo, among Nagano's colleagues, it ran into opposition from the Operations

△ *Lieutenant-Colonel James H. Doolittle. His 16 B-25 Mitchells were to cause little damage, but served to bring notice that the war could come to the heart of Japan. Besides boosting morale at home, the raid led the Japanese to adopt a strategy of further expansion to provide advanced warning of any further raids on the mainland.*

Admiral William F. Halsey, born in 1882, was the most colourful American admiral of World War II. A thrusting, ebullient personality, he was instrumental in restoring the fleet's morale in the months after Pearl Harbor. A gifted carrier commander, he nevertheless took no part in the Coral Sea fight and he went down with a skin disease shortly afterwards, being forced to hand over his Task Force 16 (*Enterprise* and *Hornet*) to Spruance for the Midway battle.

was that Doolittle and his companions were to take off some 500 miles from Japan, carry out their mission, and land in Nationalist China, deck landings by B-25's being impossible. Some 200 miles east of the area from which the planes were to take off, Halsey's force fell in with an enemy patrol and the American admiral had to order Doolittle to take off at once as the necessary secrecy could no longer be guaranteed.

A few tons of bombs were shared out between the Japanese capital and the large cities of Nagoya and Kobe from 1300 hours on April 13, but no appreciable damage was done. Of the 16 planes which took part in the raid, one landed on the aerodrome at Vladivostok and was seized by the Soviet authorities. The pilots of the remaining 15, running out of fuel, either crash landed or ordered their crews to bale out. Of the 80 crew, five were interned by the Russians, 62 were picked up by the Chinese, one was killed while descending by parachute, four drowned, and eight were taken prisoner by the Japanese. Three of these last were executed as "war criminals".

Yamamoto's views at last prevail

Before they went down under the Americans' guns, the Japanese picket trawlers met by Halsey's task force had had time to radio Tokyo. In the face of this air raid, the bitterest of humiliations for the whole Navy, there was no further disagreement over Yamamoto's plan as he went to offer his humble excuses to the Emperor. And so on May 5 the Chief of Naval Operations issued "Naval Order No. 18 of the Grand Imperial Headquarters" requiring that before June 20 the Commander of the Combined Fleet should "proceed to the occupation of Midway Island and key positions in the Western Aleutians in collaboration with the army".

Meanwhile the 4th Fleet (Vice-Admiral Inouye), suitably reinforced, was to occupy Port Moresby on the south coast of eastern New Guinea and the little island of Tulagi in the Solomon archipelago opposite Guadalcanal. At the beginning of July they were expected to seize strategic points in New Caledonia and Fiji. As we shall see, the "Australian School" had not given up its preferences, but

Yamamoto took no notice, as meanwhile the conquest of Midway would give him the chance to wipe out the American fleet.

In April, at its base in Truk in the Caroline Islands, the Japanese 4th Fleet had been reinforced by two heavy cruisers and three aircraft-carriers, two fleet ones (*Zuikaku* and *Shokaku*, 25,700 tons each) and one small (*Shoho*, 11,300 tons). Acting on orders received, Vice-Admiral Shigeyoshi Inouye divided his Task Force "MO", based on the 4th Fleet, into a Carrier Striking Force, two Invasion Groups, a Support Group, and a Covering Group. The Tulagi Invasion Group occupied its objective without opposition on May 3. On the following day 14 transport vessels of the Port Moresby Invasion Group set sail.

Moresby reinforced

Under an agreement of March 17 between London and Washington, the United States had agreed to take charge of the defence of the whole of the Pacific, including Australia and New Zealand. Alerted in time by his code-breakers,

Admiral Nimitz sent Task Force 17 (Rear-Admiral Fletcher) towards Port Moresby. The force was centred on two aircraft-carriers, *Yorktown* (Rear-Admiral Fletcher) and *Lexington* (Rear-Admiral W. Fitch) and was joined south of the Solomon Islands by an Australian task force of cruisers under Rear-Admiral J. G. Crace. The fact remains, however, that for the accomplishment of his mission Cincpac had no authority over the 300 American planes based in northern Australia and Port Moresby. These were under the Supreme Commander South-West Asia, General MacArthur, and hence there was a certain lack of co-ordination.

The ensuing actions between the opposing forces on May 6–8 came to be called the Battle of the Coral Sea. We have already remarked that the engagement marks a date in naval warfare as it was the first time that two fleets fought from over the horizon without ever being in sight of each other, and attempted to destroy each other by bombs and aerial torpedoes.

The eminent naval historian Professor Morison has called this action the "Battle of Naval Errors". He cannot be gainsaid, in view of the many mistakes committed

◁ *"Dixon to carrier: scratch one flat-top!" was the exulting message radioed back to Fletcher during the massive American air strikes which overwhelmed the diminutive Japanese carrier* Shoho *during the battle of the Coral Sea.* Shoho *never had a chance, and the American planes swarming round her are clearly shown in the identifying rings.*
△ *Perhaps more important than* Shoho's *destruction was the serious damage done to the big Japanese fleet carrier* Shokaku *in the Coral Sea fight. She would not be ready for the deciding battle at Midway; nor would her sister ship* Zuikaku, *whose air group suffered crippling losses.*

◁ *Revenge for the Japanese:*
Lexington, *listing and ablaze*
after the fierce internal
explosions which made it essential
for her crew to abandon ship.
A damaged carrier was terribly
vulnerable to belated explosions,
long after enemy attack; for
fumes always tended to build up
and unless full precautions were
taken could reach a lethal level.
Draining the fuel lines and
filling them with carbon dioxide
proved one of the best safeguards.
▽ *One of the last explosions*
aboard the doomed Lexington.

by the airmen on both sides, errors both in navigation and in the identification of the enemy's ships, as well as in the assessment of aerial bombing and torpedoing. In their defence, however, it must be pointed out that rapidly alternating sunshine and heavy squalls over the Coral Sea could not have made their task easy. Tactically, success went to the Japanese, since against the loss of the light carrier *Shoho*, one destroyer, one minelayer, and three minesweepers, they sank the American *Lexington* (33,000 tons), the oiler *Neosho*, which they took for another aircraft-carrier, and the destroyer *Sims*.

"The *Yorktown*, which came first under attack, successfully evaded the torpedoes launched at her and took only a single bomb hit, which did not significantly impair her fighting effectiveness. But the *Lexington*, larger and less manoeuvrable, fell victim to an 'anvil' attack on both bows simultaneously and took two torpedoes on the port side, which flooded three boiler rooms. Two bomb hits, received at almost the same time, inflicted only minor damage. The list caused by the torpedo hits was quickly corrected by shifting oil. Her engines were unharmed, and her speed did not fall below 24 knots.

"But at 1445 there was a severe explosion. Fires passed rapidly out of control and the carrier was forced to call for assistance. The *Yorktown* took aboard the *Lexington* planes that were in the air, but there was no opportunity to transfer those already on the *Lexington*. With the ship burning furiously and shaken by frequent explosions there was no choice but to 'get the men off'."

Strategically, however, the advantage was on the Allies' side, as the serious damage done to *Shokaku* and the losses of the aircraft from *Zuikaku* forced Inouye to give up the idea of landing at Port Moresby.

Worse still, the several detachments of the Combined Fleet had to set off for Midway and the Aleutians by May 26 and it was not possible, in the short time available, either to repair *Shokaku* or to replace the aircraft lost by *Zuikaku*. On the other hand, the Japanese grossly exaggerated their successes. They claimed that *Yorktown* had met the same fate as *Lexington*, whereas she had been hit by only one 800-lb bomb. Hence the "spirit of imprudence and error" which seized Yamamoto. This is shown by the war game, or map exercise, carried out to test out Operation "Midway" The director of the exercise,

Rear-Admiral Ugaki, did not hesitate to cancel such decisions by the referee as seemed to him unfavourable to the Japanese side.

However, until the ships yet to be built under the American budgets of 1939 to 1941 came into service, the Japanese fleet enjoyed considerable superiority over its enemy. This is shown in the table at right, in which we give only the ships which took part in the actions of June 3–6 between Midway Atoll and Dutch Harbor in the Aleutians.

The Japanese aircraft-carriers had between them 410 planes, those of Admiral Nimitz 233. But Nimitz could also call upon the 115 concentrated on the airstrips at Midway in case of enemy attack. Yet these figures must not make us lose sight of the fact that the American inferiority in ships and planes was not only quantitative but qualitative as well. The Grumann F4F Wildcat fighters were less manoeuvrable and had a slower rate of climb than the Japanese Mitsubishi A6M Zeros. The torpedo bomber then in service with the U.S. Navy, the Douglas TBD-1 Devastator, with a top speed of only 206 mph, was entirely at the mercy of the Zero, Japan's standard carrier-borne fighter, which could reach some 340 mph. Also, the American air-dropped 21-inch torpedo was so slow to reach its target that the victim had a good chance of taking avoiding action. It is nevertheless true that the Japanese Commander-in-Chief threw away recklessly the enormous chances which, for the last time, his numerical and *matériel* superiority gave him.

△ *Crewmen from the "Lady Lex" are hauled aboard a rescue ship. Many of* Lexington's *crew members were in tears as she went down, being "plank owners"—men who had served with the ship since she had been commissioned.*

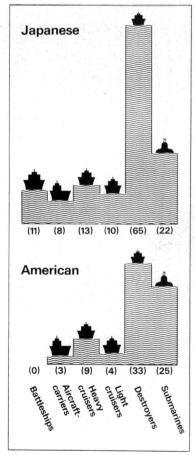

Japanese

(11) (8) (13) (10) (65) (22)

American

(0) (3) (9) (4) (33) (25)

Battleships
Aircraft-carriers
Heavy cruisers
Light cruisers
Destroyers
Submarines

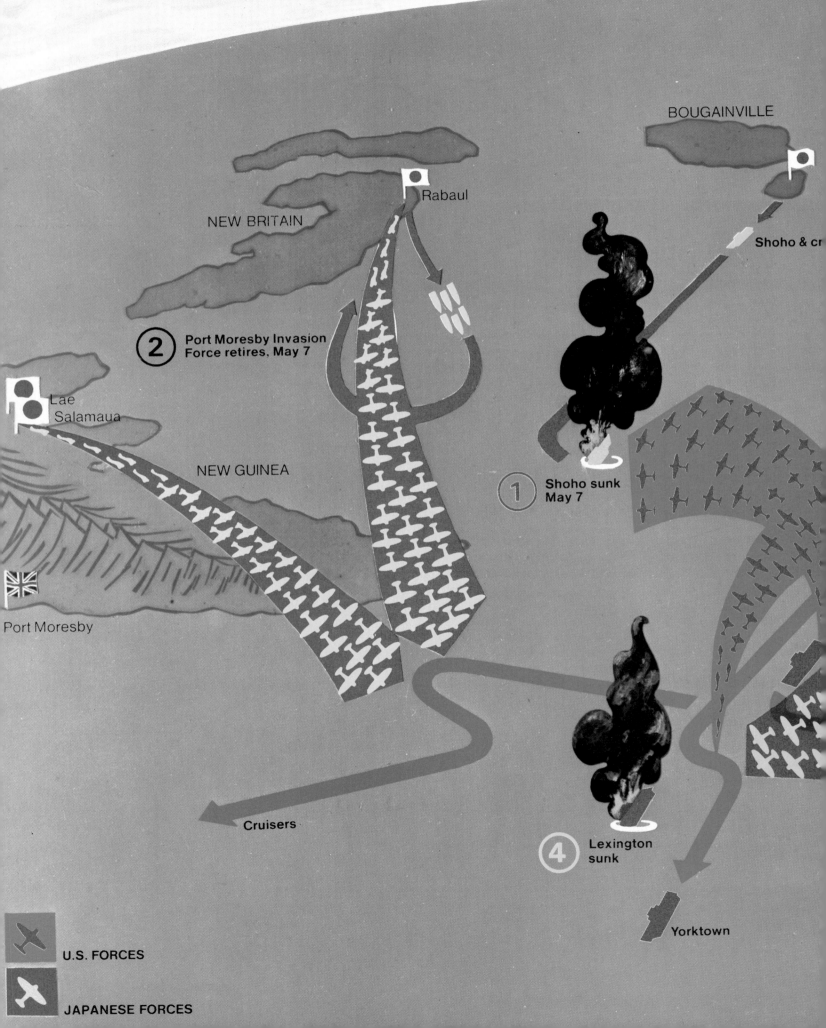

CORAL SEA:
THE FIRST CARRIER v. CARRIER DUEL

BOUGAINVILLE

Rabaul

NEW BRITAIN

Shoho & cr

② Port Moresby Invasion
Force retires, May 7

Lae
Salamaua

NEW GUINEA

① Shoho sunk
May 7

Port Moresby

Cruisers

④ Lexington
sunk

Yorktown

U.S. FORCES

JAPANESE FORCES

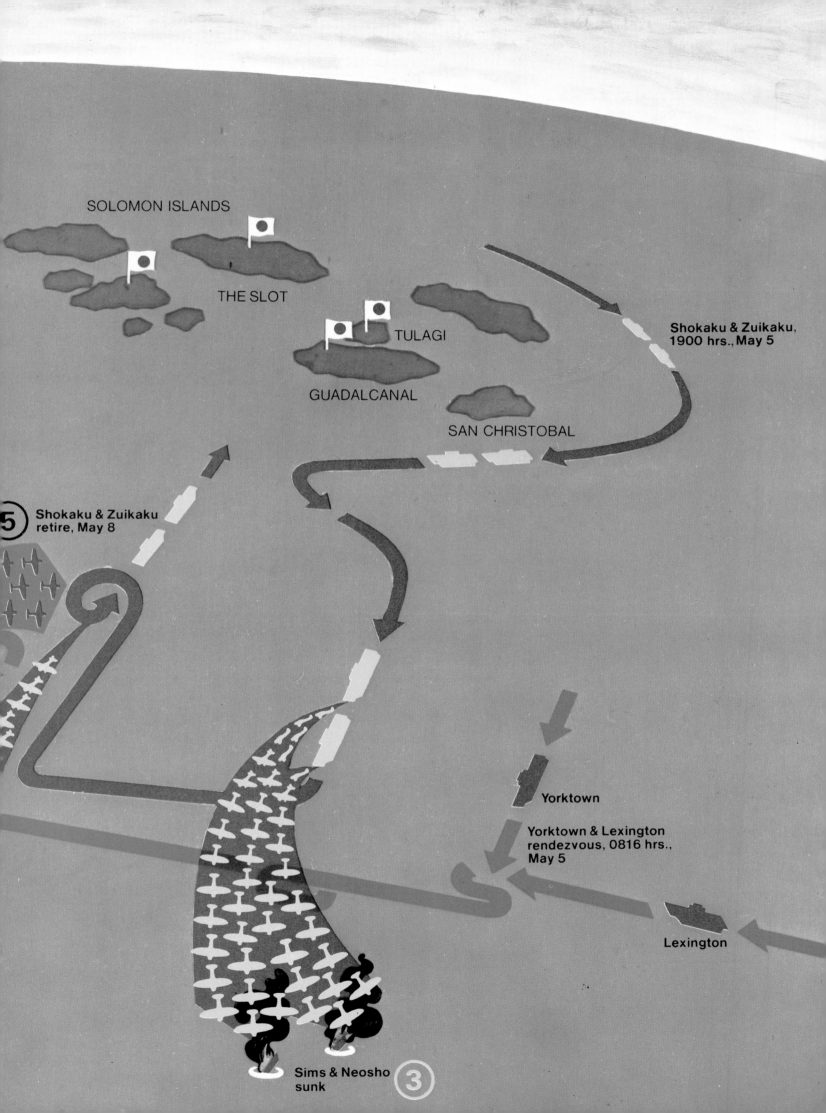

SOLOMON ISLANDS

THE SLOT

TULAGI

GUADALCANAL

SAN CHRISTOBAL

Shokaku & Zuikaku,
1900 hrs., May 5

5 Shokaku & Zuikaku
retire, May 8

Yorktown

Yorktown & Lexington
rendezvous, 0816 hrs.,
May 5

Lexington

Sims & Neosho
sunk

3

CHAPTER 77
MIDWAY: the showdown

For the operation designed to seize the islands of Attu and Kiska in the Aleutians, Yamamoto assembled a task force whose lavish size was out of all proportion to the strategic value of the objective: three heavy cruisers, three light cruisers, 13 destroyers, and the aircraft-carriers *Ryujo* and *Junyo* with between them 82 planes on board. In view of the impending threat to this theatre, however, the Americans sent out five cruisers and 13 destroyers (Task Force 8) under Rear-Admiral R. A. Theobald.

A worse feature of the Japanese organisation, and one less easy to explain, however, was the fact that within the main strength of the Combined Fleet which was to secure the occupation of Midway and, it was hoped, the destruction of the American fleet at the same time, the task forces were so loosely co-ordinated that they were quite unable to support each other within the narrow time limits available. Thus everything was decided on June 4 between Vice-Admiral Nagumo's four aircraft-carriers (272 planes) and Rear-Admirals Fletcher and R. A. Spruance's three (233 planes) supported by the 115 planes from Midway. On the decisive day nine battleships, including the colossal 64,200-ton *Yamato*, 11 cruisers, and 32 destroyers never fired a shot and the 41 planes on board the light aircraft-carriers *Zuiho* and *Hosho* took no part in the action.

This is not to say that Yamamoto's logic was at fault: the bombardment of Midway on June 4 and the assault on the atoll next day would provoke Nimitz into bringing out his fleet so that the engagement at sea, all being well, would take place on June 7 or 8. This would give Nagumo time to recover his liberty of action and the Japanese Commander-in-Chief to draw in his scattered forces. To leave nothing to chance, on June 2 two squadrons of submarines were to station themselves along all the routes the Americans might take on their way to assist Midway. Logical this might have been, but there was a basic error in its reasoning, as Professor Morison has pointed out:

"The vital defect in this sort of plan is that it depends on the enemy's doing exactly what is expected. If he is smart enough to do something different—in this case to have fast carriers on the spot—the operation is thrown into confusion."

But Yamamoto had no idea that the enemy was reading over his shoulder what amounted to an open book.

△ The target: Midway Atoll, outrider of the Hawaiian chain, two insignificant specks of land with their vital airfield.

▷ The long arm of the Midway air defences: a B-17 Fortress takes off for a long-range sweep. When the Japanese came down on Midway they found that the Americans had learned the lessons of Pearl Harbor and the Philippines. Not a plane was caught on the ground by the first Japanese air strike.

Rochefort's ruse

There was a somewhat tense atmosphere in Pearl Harbor in spite of the breaking of the Japanese codes. Men began to wonder if in fact they were not getting involved in some diabolical deception about the objective of the next Japanese move. Their last doubts were dispelled by a ruse thought up by Commander J. Rochefort, head of the Combat Intelligence Unit at Pearl Harbor: the commander in each of the areas where a Japanese attack might be expected was required to signal some deficiency in his equipment. The Midway commander chose his seawater distillation plant, and a few days later the Americans intercepted a report from a Japanese listening post announcing that it had heard "AF" report such a deficiency. "AF" had been mentioned as the objective of Japan's present move, and Rochefort now knew for certain that Midway was the target about to be attacked.

The whole archipelago of Hawaii had been in a state of alert against a landing ever since May 14. The little Sand and Eastern Islands, the only land surfaces of any size in Midway Atoll, were rightly the object of particular care and attention and were so well reinforced with A.A. guns, reconnaissance planes, and fighter planes that the commanders on Midway, Commander Cyril T. Simard and Marine Lieutenant-Colonel Harold Shannon (soon promoted to Captain and Colonel respectively) had just over 3,000 men and 115 planes under them.

Nimitz's ambush

Not counting Rear-Admiral Theobald's squadron, Admiral Nimitz's forces were divided into two groups:

Task Force 16, based on the aircraft-carriers *Enterprise* and *Hornet,* together with six cruisers and nine destroyers. Vice-Admiral Halsey was now in hospital and so command of this force was given to Rear-Admiral Raymond A. Spruance, whose intellectual powers were so formidable as to earn him the nickname of "electric brain".

Task Force 17, still under the command of Rear-Admiral F. J. Fletcher, based on the aircraft-carrier *Yorktown,* to-gether with two cruisers and five destroyers. The damage sustained by *Yorktown* on the previous May 8 would have taken two months to repair in peacetime. The 1,400 men of the Pearl Harbor dockyards did it in less than 46 hours. This allowed Fletcher to set sail in the morning of May 30, behind Task Force 16 which had left on May 28.

And so when the Japanese submarines, which were behind schedule anyway, reached the watching stations assigned to them, Admiral Nimitz's ships had already gone, and they were thus unable to report the enemy's dispositions or strength. On June 3 at 0900 hours, when the first enemy sighting reports reached them, Fletcher and Spruance were north-east of Midway and in a good position to act against the enemy should he attack the atoll. On

Patching up the "Old Lady" at Pearl Harbor. It should have taken months to repair the damage suffered by Yorktown *at the Coral Sea—but under Nimitz's goading she was made seaworthy again in an incredibly short time—well under 48 hours.*

leaving Pearl Harbor they had received the following warning from Cincpac in anticipation of the enemy's superior strength:

"You will be governed by the principle of calculated risk, which you shall interpret to mean the avoidance of exposure of your force to attack by superior enemy forces without good prospect of inflicting, as a result of such exposure, greater damage on the enemy."

But as Professor Potter and Admiral Nimitz point out, "to fight cautiously, to meet a superior enemy force without unduly exposing one's own is difficult in the highest degree. That Fletcher and Spruance were able to carry out these orders successfully was due primarily to their skilful exploitation of intelligence, which enabled them to turn the element of surprise against the Japanese."

△ *American torpedo bombers ranged on the flight deck of* Enterprise. *These planes are from Torpedo Squadron 6, and only four of them came back. The TBD bomber was a death-trap: sluggish, lumbering, and fatally vulnerable to enemy fighter attack.*

▷ *Revenge for the Japanese:* Hiryu's *bombers hit* Yorktown. *This picture shows the fire raging on her flight deck; but the* Hiryu *bomb which did most damage went clean through the flight, hangar, and second decks and exploded in the funnel uptakes, stopping the ship dead and forcing Admiral Fletcher to shift his flag to the cruiser* Astoria.

now at sea or about to set sail. Should Nagumo, sailing on more than 600 miles ahead of *Yamato*, be alerted? This would mean breaking the sacrosanct radio silence and Yamamoto could not bring himself to do it, although the Americans already seemed to have penetrated the secret of Operation Midway. In such a situation the Germans would have said "*Wirkung geht vor Tarnung*", or "effectiveness comes before camouflage".

Battle in the sky

It was shortly after 0900 on June 3 when the first contact with the enemy was reported. A Catalina searching 470 miles to the south-west of Midway had been fired on by two Japanese patrol craft. Further confirmation that the Japanese were moving on Midway came when another Catalina spotted the convoy and escorts of the Midway Occupation Force.

In Walter Lord's words:

"Farther to the west, Ensign Jack Reid piloted another PBY across an empty ocean. He had started earlier than the rest, was now 700 miles from Midway, nearing the end of his outward leg. So far, nothing worth reporting. With the PBY on automatic pilot, Reid again studied the sea with his binoculars. Still nothing—occasional cloud puffs and a light haze hung over the Pacific, but not enough to bother him. It was shortly before 9:25 A.M., and Ensign Reid was a man with no problems at all.

"Suddenly he looked, then looked again. Thirty miles dead ahead he could make out dark objects along the horizon. Ships, lots of them, all heading toward him. Handing the glasses to his co-pilot Ensign Hardeman, he calmly asked, 'Do you see what I see?'

"Hardeman took one look: 'You are damned right I do.'

"Commander Yasumi Toyama looked up from his charts on the bridge of the light cruiser *Jintsu*. For once all the transports were keeping in column, but the destroyer on the port side forward was raising a fuss. She hoisted a signal, then fired a smoke shell. Toyama rushed out on the bridge wing, and there was no need to ask what had happened. Everyone was looking and pointing. There, low and well out of range on the horizon, hovered a PBY."

That afternoon the convoy was attacked by a formation of Flying Fortresses.

Even before the Japanese fleet left its bases, Rear-Admiral Ryunosuke Kusaka, Nagumo's chief-of-staff, made the following observation to Yamamoto: so as not to hinder take-off and landing on the flight decks, the aircraft-carriers had had their masts shortened to such an extent that their radio aerials were incapable of intercepting any enemy wireless traffic. Thus the carrier forces which would be the first to make contact would be deprived of an essential source of information. It was therefore suggested that the battleship *Yamato* should accompany the aircraft-carriers, but this was rejected by the Commander-in-Chief.

Even so, the Japanese admiral's flagship intercepted in the single day of June 1 180 messages from Hawaii, 72 of which were classified "urgent". This sudden intensification of radio traffic, as well as the great increase in aerial reconnaissance, could mean that the enemy forces were

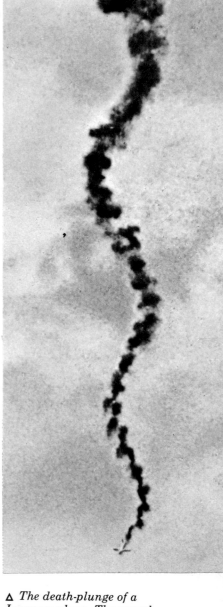

△ *The death-plunge of a Japanese plane. The superb Zero, although far and away the best fighter in the Pacific theatre at the time of Midway, was nevertheless a comparatively easy victim— if it could be held in the gun sights at the right moment. It lacked armour plate protection, and tended to explode readily when hit in the tanks.*

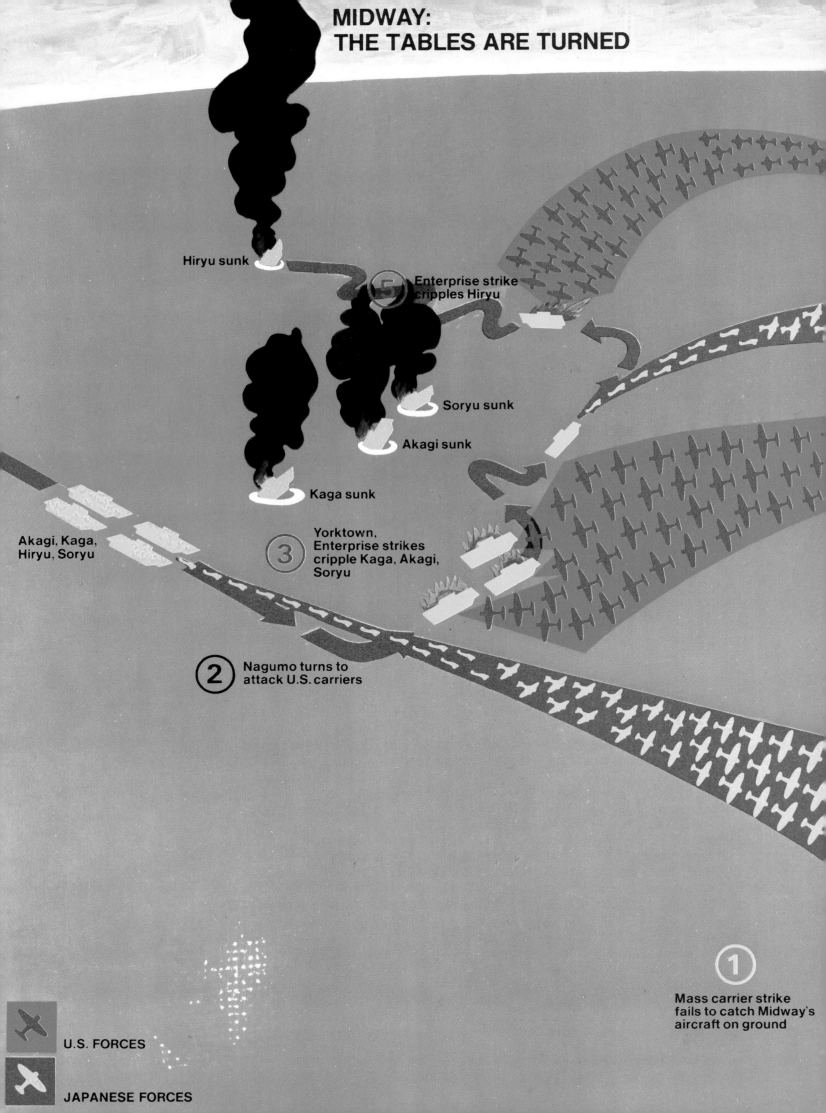

MIDWAY:
THE TABLES ARE TURNED

Hiryu sunk

Enterprise strike
cripples Hiryu

Soryu sunk

Akagi sunk

Kaga sunk

Akagi, Kaga,
Hiryu, Soryu

Yorktown,
Enterprise strikes
cripple Kaga, Akagi,
Soryu

③

② Nagumo turns to
attack U.S. carriers

①

Mass carrier strike
fails to catch Midway's
aircraft on ground

U.S. FORCES

JAPANESE FORCES

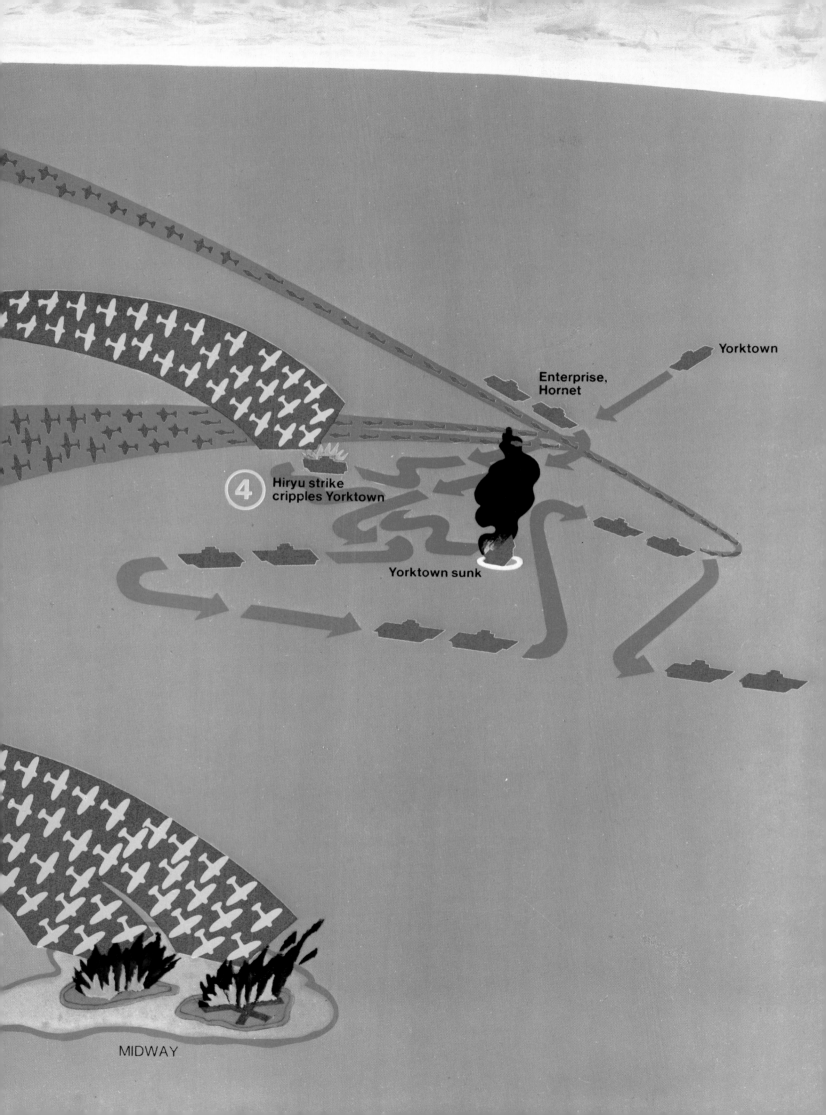

Yorktown

Enterprise,
Hornet

④ Hiryu strike
cripples Yorktown

Yorktown sunk

MIDWAY

At dawn Nagumo had reached a position 280 miles north-west of his objective and turned his force into the wind. Then the carriers *Akagi, Kaga, Hiryu,* and *Soryu* unleashed 36 level bombers, 36 dive-bombers, and 36 fighters. At the same time six seaplanes took off to reconnoitre for American warships, followed half an hour later by a seventh, delayed by a breakdown in the catapult gear on the cruiser *Tone.*

Captain Simard got the alert in time to put up all his airworthy planes, but his 26 fighters were no match for the Japanese Zeros, which knocked out 17 of them and crippled seven others to such an extent that they had to be written off. The Japanese lost only six. The Midway air force was not silenced for all that. Lieutenant Joichi Tomonaga, who led the first wave, signalled back to Nagumo that in his opinion a second attack was necessary.

The Japanese admiral acted on Tomonaga's report and ordered that the torpedo-carrying bombers of the second wave (108 planes), armed to attack any U.S. ships that might appear, should have their torpedoes replaced by bombs, and the level bombers their armour-piercing bombs by high-explosive ones. This decision seemed justified by the ferocity of the Midway air force's counter-attack. It is true that Captain Simard's pilots pressed their charges home, as the saying was in the days of cavalry; it is also true that the training of the men on the one side and the efficiency of the machines on the other were unequal to the courage displayed. Thirty-nine torpedo-carrying aircraft and dive-bombers had attacked the Japanese without causing any damage to their ships; 17 of these planes had been shot down and seven were declared beyond repair on their return. A squadron of Flying Fortresses then bombed the enemy convoy from a height of 21,000 feet, also without success. Though these attacks had been fruitless, Admiral Nagumo nevertheless threw in his second wave of fighters.

Heavy U.S. losses

Meanwhile, at 0728 hours, *Tone's* seaplane signalled that it had spotted ten enemy ships 240 miles away, steaming south-south-east. Not until 0820 hours did the pilot see, and then only vaguely, that there was an aircraft-carrier with them. Though this report was far from clear, it put Nagumo in a very embarrassing position. If he sent up his second wave dive-bombers (36 planes) to attack this formation, they would be without fighter escort and would take a heavy beating. The same danger faced *Akagi's* and *Kaga's* torpedo-bombers, which were now loaded with bombs instead of torpedoes. These were less likely to be successful against warships. If he waited for the first wave to land on his carriers when they returned from Midway he would then be able to attack with all his forces. And so at 0855 hours Nagumo signalled his squadron: "After landing, formation will proceed north provisionally. We expect to make contact with the enemy and destroy him."

Whereupon the armourers of the air-craft-carriers again threw themselves into the task of changing the weapons on the aircraft, replacing H.E. bombs with torpedoes and armour-piercing bombs. As time was short, they piled up the bombs alongside the aircraft in the hangars.

The first U.S. Navy squadron to attack, 15 TBD Devastator torpedo-bombers under Lieutenant-Commander John Waldron, from *Hornet,* appeared at about 0930, skimming over the tops of the waves. A few minutes later they had all been shot down and only one out of their total crew of 30 survived. The Japanese authors of *Midway. The Battle that doomed Japan,* Mitsuo Fuchida and Masatake Okumiya, describe this unsuccessful but heroic action:

"The first enemy carrier planes to attack were 15 torpedo bombers. When first spotted by our screening ships and combat air patrol, they were still not visible from the carriers, but they soon appeared as tiny dark specks in the sky, a little above the horizon, on *Akagi's* starboard bow. The distant wings flashed in the sun. Occasionally one of the specks burst into a spark of flame and trailed black smoke as it fell into the water. Our fighters were on the job, and the enemy again seemed to be without fighter protection.

"Presently a report came in from a Zero group leader: 'All 15 enemy torpedo bombers shot down.' Nearly 50 Zeros had gone to intercept the unprotected enemy formation! Small wonder that it did not get through."

The squadrons of Devastator torpedo-bombers from *Enterprise* and *Yorktown* were almost as unfortunate: they lost 20

out of 26 planes to the Japanese fighters and A.A. guns. Worse still, not a single one of their torpedoes reached its target.

So by 1015 hours Nagumo was winning. At the cost of six of his own planes he had destroyed 83 of his enemy's and at 1030 hours he would unleash on the American squadron a wave of 102 planes, including 54 torpedo-bombers and 36 dive-bombers, in which he put his full confidence.

By 1028 hours, however, the Rising Sun had been decisively defeated.

A change of fortune

At 0552 hours on June 4 a message to Admirals Fletcher and Spruance announced that the enemy forces with four aircraft-carriers were 230 miles to their south-west. Fletcher, the senior of the two officers and therefore in command of the whole force, gave the order to attack. From 0702 hours Task Force 16, now sailing towards the enemy, sent up 116 planes. *Yorktown,* in Task Force 17, waited until 0838 hours before launching her 35.

It has been said that Rear-Admiral

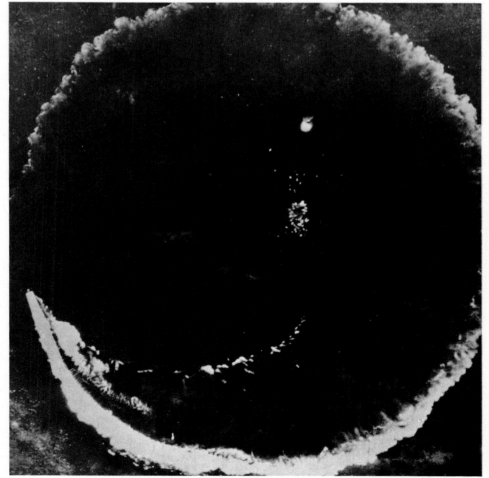

△ *The shattered wreck of the Japanese cruiser* Mikuma. *She had been retiring from Midway when she collided with* Mogami, *and as the two cruisers limped on in the wake of Kurita's other cruisers they were set upon by an American air strike. On the wrecked rear turret can be seen the remains of Captain Fleming's Vindicator bomber, which he deliberately crashed on the target when he was fatally hit during his bombing run. Further attacks late on June 5 finished off* Mikuma.

Spruance had calculated the time so as to surprise the enemy aircraft-carriers just when their flight-decks would be cluttered up with planes returning from Midway. With admirable, almost unprecedented modesty he himself has denied the flattering legend in his preface to Commanders Fuchida's and Okumiya's book:

"When I read the account of the events of June 4, 1942 I am struck once more by the part played by chance in warfare. The authors congratulate us on having chosen the moment of our attack on the Japanese aircraft-carriers when they were at their most vulnerable, that is with their flight-decks encumbered with planes ready to take off. We did not choose this moment deliberately. For my part I had only the feeling that we had to achieve surprise and strike the enemy planes with all the strength at our command as soon as we met them."

It can only be said that the war leader who puts into practice the principle enunciated by Napoleon: "Action! Action! Speed!" can never go wrong.

The approach of the American planes was not without its difficulties, as the position they had been given was erroneous, the Japanese ships having changed direction. This caused an unwelcome detour. Some Wildcat fighter squadrons lost the torpedo-carrying aircraft they were supposed to be escorting. The massacre described above was the result. But the heroic sacrifice of Waldron and his men payed off a few minutes later. The Zero fighters were so busy tracking down Waldron's planes at low level that they were too late to prevent an attack by Douglas SBD Dauntlesses, which dive-bombed the Japanese aircraft-carriers from a height of nearly 20,000 feet. On the carriers themselves, the Japanese were too busy warding off torpedoes to see the second attack.

The scene has been described by an eye-witness on the flight-deck of the ill-fated *Akagi*:

"I looked up to see three black enemy planes plummeting towards our ship. Some of our machine guns managed to fire a few frantic bursts at them, but it was too late. The plump silhouettes of the American 'Dauntless' dive-bombers grew larger, and then a number of black objects suddenly floated eerily from their wings. Bombs! Down they came straight towards me! I fell intuitively to the deck and crawled behind a command post mantlet.

"The terrifying scream of the dive bombers reached me first, followed by the crashing explosion of a direct hit. There was a blinding flash and then a second explosion, much louder than the first. I was shaken by a weird blast of warm air. There was still another shock, but less severe, apparently a near-miss. Then followed a startling quiet as the barking of guns suddenly ceased. I got up and looked at the sky. The enemy planes were already gone from sight . . .

"Looking about, I was horrified at the destruction that had been wrought in a matter of seconds. There was a huge hole in the flight deck just behind the amidships elevator. The elevator itself, twisted like molten glass, was drooping into the hangar. Deck plates reeled upwards in grotesque configurations. Planes stood tail up, belching livid flame and jet black smoke. Reluctant tears streamed down my cheeks as I watched the fires spread."

Nagumo's force destroyed

A few minutes later a series of explosions from petrol and the loose piles of bombs rocked the huge ship from stem to stern, causing widespread fires and destruction. Akagi's radio was out of action, and Vice-Admiral Nagumo and his staff left the ship at 1046 hours.

"As the number of dead and wounded increased and the fires got further out of control, Captain Aoki finally decided at 1800 that the ship must be abandoned. The injured were lowered into boats and cutters sent alongside by the screening destroyers. Many uninjured men leapt into the sea and swam away from the stricken ship. Destroyers Arashi and Nowaki picked up all survivors. When the rescue work was complete, Captain Aoki radioed to Admiral Nagumo at 1920 from one of the destroyers, asking permission to sink the crippled carrier. This inquiry was monitored by the combined fleet flagship, whence Admiral Yamamoto dispatched an order at 2225 to delay the carrier's disposition. Upon receipt of this instruction, the captain returned to his carrier alone. He reached the anchor deck, which was still free from fire, and there lashed himself to an anchor . . ."

A few miles away, Kaga, hit by four bombs, had also become a raging inferno and her crew were attempting to control the flames amidst explosions which were causing widespread death and destruction. The ship had been attacked by Enterprise's and Hornet's Dauntless dive-bomber squadrons, led by Lieutenant-Commander Clarence W. McClusky. Soryu was bombed by planes led by Lieutenant-Commander Maxwell Leslie and by formations from Yorktown. By 1040 hours Soryu's rudder and engines were out of action and her crew was surrounded by fires and explosions.

The only unit of the Japanese Carrier Striking Force now fit to fight was Hiryu. In accordance with Nagumo's order she sent off some 40 planes in two waves to attack Task Force 17. At mid-day, 18 dive-bombers appeared above Yorktown. The American fighters, warned in time by radar, and the A.A. wiped out 12 of them, but two bombs reached their target and the powerful vessel was brought to a standstill at 1220 hours. She had got under way again, but not at full speed, when Hiryu's aircraft pressed home their attack

△ Hiryu escaped the first shattering dive-bomber attack which knocked out Kaga, Akagi, and Soryu – but not for long. Here her blazing and abandoned hulk wallows sluggishly in a calm sea. She finally sank around 0915 on June 5.

through a seemingly impenetrable barrage of fire and scored hits with two torpedoes. Seeing his ship in danger of capsizing, her commander ordered her to be abandoned and taken in tow. This was to be *Hiryu*'s last action. Only 15 of her planes, including six fighters, returned. At 1630 hours, Spruance sighted her and sent in 24 Dauntlesses under McClusky. The Japanese vessel whipped her speed up to 33 knots, but she was hit by four bombs at 1700 hours. All the planes on the flight deck were set on fire and all means of escape from the ship were cut off. At dusk Task Force 16 set course eastwards as Spruance did not care to risk a night battle with an enemy force containing the battleships *Haruna* and *Kirishima,* against which he was clearly at a disadvantage.

Between 1900 and 1930 hours, *Soryu* and *Kaga* both disappeared beneath the waters of the Pacific. In the morning of the following day Nagumo, with the authority of Admiral Yamamoto, finished off the wrecks of *Akagi* and *Hiryu* with torpedoes. The commander of the second, Rear-Admiral Tamon Yamaguchi, obstinately refused to leave his ship and, to ensure that he went down with her, tied himself to the bridge.

Yamamoto gives up

On board *Yamato*, the Commander-in-Chief of the Combined Fleet could do no more than admit his powerlessness to redeem the situation now that his various detachments were so widely scattered. After a series of orders and counter-orders, on June 5 he finally confirmed the abandonment of operations against Midway and the return to their bases of his several detachments.

This was not to be done without further loss, however. In the 7th Cruiser Division, *Mogami* was in collision during the night with *Mikuma*. Hounded by enemy planes in the daylight, the former was further damaged and put out of action for a year. The latter went down at about noon on June 6. A few hours later the Japanese submarine *I-168* (Lieutenant-Commander Yahachi Tanabe), which had shelled Midway in the night of June 4–5, surprised *Yorktown* as she was being towed slowly back to Pearl Harbor. Manoeuvring swiftly and decisively it sank her with two torpedoes and cut the destroyer *Hamman* in half with a third.

This was the end of one of the most decisive battles of World War II, the effects of which were felt far beyond the waters of the Pacific. It deprived Japan of her freedom of action and it allowed the two Anglo-Saxon powers to go ahead with their policy of "Germany first", as agreed between Churchill and Roosevelt.

As well as the ships mentioned above, the Americans lost 307 dead and 147 planes. The Japanese losses of 3,500 dead and 332 planes deprived her of the cream of her naval air forces. The results show that, though they had been dealt a worse hand than the enemy, Nimitz, Fletcher, and Spruance had played their cards better than Yamamoto and Nagumo. Chance had played her part too, though. What would have happened if *Tone*'s seaplane had not been half an hour late in taking off? We shall never know.

On June 6–7 the Japanese occupied the undefended islands of Kiska and Attu in the Aleutians.

CHAPTER 78
TORCH: the American viewpoint
by Martin Blumenson

Some people still believe that President Roosevelt favoured an invasion of North Africa solely because he thought that a military success by American troops would enhance his Democratic Party's showing in the Congressional elections on November 3, 1943. Although it is true that he hoped "Torch", as the invasion was called, would take place before the voting, the amphibious forces involved had to delay their departures for North

Africa, mainly because they awaited delivery of landing ships and craft; they came ashore on November 8, five days after the elections. Yet the President never put pressure on his military leaders to launch the operation before it was ready.

Actually, there were sounder reasons why the President approved the landings. The most important consideration was probably his wish to indicate to the

▽ *American infantry storm ashore from a landing craft during a training exercise. The United States had managed to mobilise and train a vast number of men in the course of 1942, but the provision of matériel had proved more difficult. Thus a considerable number of landing craft had to be borrowed from Great Britain for Operation "Torch".*

△ *Field-Marshal Sir John Dill, head of the British Joint Staff Mission in the United States. An able strategist, he had taken over as Chief of the Imperial General Staff from Sir Edmund Ironside in 1940, but was in turn succeeded by Brooke in November 1941, when his cautious views fell foul of Churchill's overriding desires for offensive action. He had a high regard for America's military potential, and served both countries well until his death late in 1944.*

△ *Henry Stimson, U.S. Secretary of War, a staunch supporter of the Compulsory Service Act of September 1940, which gave the United States a sound beginning in building up her armed forces for the inevitable war ahead.*

Russians, who were under extreme duress in 1942, that the Anglo-American members of the Grand Alliance fighting the Axis nations were making an active contribution to the war effort. In all the discussions revolving around strategic decisions, the Western Allies consistently sought to assist the Russians by taking action that would draw German forces away from the Eastern Front.

Roosevelt, moreover, wished to demonstrate the feasibility of combined Anglo-American operations. He hoped to transmit at once the close co-operation and mutual high regard that existed on the highest levels of government to the armed forces of both nations. Making coalition ventures work was a vital prerequisite for eventual victory, and the sooner they started, the better were the chances for quick development of coalition unity and *esprit*.

Finally, the President wished to divert the interest and the will of the American people, stunned and shocked by the Japanese attack on Pearl Harbor, from the Pacific area and to arouse and direct their attention to the European side of the conflict. For even before the United States were at war, Roosevelt and his strategic advisers had decided in conversations with British military officials that if the country became involved in war against the Axis, the United States would follow a "Germany first" strategy, as we have seen. In other words, the United States would remain on the defensive against Japan while exerting every effort to crush the military forces of Germany and Italy first. Among the factors supporting this policy was the logistical fact that it took many more ships to maintain forces in the Pacific than it did in the Atlantic.

Thus, offensive operations were required in Europe. The best way to commit American energies to that part of the war was to have an early meeting with the European enemies.

The direct approach

According to American strategic thought and doctrine, the most appropriate method to defeat an enemy was by the direct approach: grapple with the main enemy forces and crush them in battle. Applied to the situation in Europe, this meant coming to grips with and concen-

trating against Germany first. To do this, Allied troops had to enter upon the European continent. A quick and crushing victory over Germany would bring about the surrender of Italy. The Americans could then turn to the Pacific and eliminate Japan.

From the beginning, this was, in essence, the strategic concept of General George C. Marshall. Although he constantly sought to implement his view, the desires of the British and the condition of the American military establishment would dictate a postponement of what has come to be regarded as the American strategic approach.

No sooner had Pearl Harbor brought America into the war than Churchill and some of his advisers travelled to Washington, D.C., to confer with the President and his military officials. In a series of talks in December 1941 and January 1942, known as the "Arcadia" Conference, Churchill discovered to his immense relief that the Americans had no intention of adopting anything but a "Germany first" strategy. Marshall reiterated that Germany was the main enemy and "the key to victory". His principal assistant, Dwight D. Eisenhower, said: "We've got to go to Europe and fight . . . we've got to begin slugging with air at West Europe; to be followed by land attack as soon as possible."

The commitment was heartening to Churchill, but the enthusiasm to fight the Germans immediately seemed unrealistic. For the American military forces were in the process of expanding, organising, and training for combat; they were hardly a match for a strong and veteran foe, particularly in major operations. According to Sir John Dill, the United States "has not–repeat not–the slightest conception of what the war means, and their armed forces are more unready for war than it is possible to imagine".

In these circumstances Churchill, before returning home, spoke somewhat vaguely of the possibility of launching a relatively small Anglo-American operation in Norway. He also suggested landings in French North Africa, a plan he codenamed "Gymnast".

The Americans saw these as diversionary efforts that would interfere with a quick strike against Germany. As early as February 1942, Eisenhower outlined the American strategic objectives as being to maintain the present position in the Pacific and "to develop in conjunction

with the British a definite plan for operations against North West Europe". What was required, he believed, was an American build-up of resources–men and *matériel*–in the United Kingdom, followed by an Anglo-American cross-Channel attack in 1942.

Roosevelt's mediation

But Roosevelt, perhaps better than his military chiefs, estimated that American forces could not hope to carry out a programme of this sort. Like the British, he thought that a cross-Channel attack of any size could not be mounted probably until 1943. He talked of joining the British in the Middle East or the Mediterranean.

To resolve the differences in outlook between him and his military strategists, Roosevelt directed Harry Hopkins, his close adviser, and Marshall to go to London to confer with Churchill and his military staff. As the result of discussions in April, the coalition partners tentatively agreed on "Bolero", codename for building up a concentration of American

forces and supplies in the United Kingdom; on "Round-up", an eventual cross-Channel attack of major proportions; and on "Sledgehammer", a limited attack in 1942 to seize a bridgehead in France.

All firmly recognised the need for "Bolero", and indeed U.S. forces were already beginning to arrive in Northern Ireland, but the British had serious reservations with respect to the other ventures, primarily because they would have to shoulder a preponderant portion of the burden. The United States, it was estimated, could have ready and available for action in 1942 no more than three and a half combat divisions. This was hardly enough for what was being contemplated.

Even Eisenhower, who was sent to confer with British authorities on establishing the arrangements for "Bolero", had to agree that cross-Channel operations in 1942 were impractical. The spring of 1943 was more likely. Nevertheless, if there was ever to be a cross-Channel invasion, "Bolero" had to be implemented, and late in June 1942, Marshall appointed Eisenhower to be Commanding General, European Theatre of Operations, U.S. Army. His task was to make sure that American forces shipped to the

△ *Cadets at the passing out ceremony at West Point Military Academy. Soon their training and the theories of war on which it was based would be put to the acid test of war against Germany and Japan, two experienced and able adversaries.*

△ *The U.S. Army in training: infantry rush a light jeep-towed gun ashore. Through a careful build-up from basic training to divisional manoeuvres, the American fighting man was given a thorough training in the amphibious warfare that was to be so much a feature of U.S. operations during the war.*

United Kingdom would be ready, trained, and supplied when the decision was reached to invade the continent and engage the Germans.

About that time, Churchill arrived in Washington for additional strategic discussions. Having concluded that major attacks were impossible in the near future, he recommended "preparing within the general structure of 'Bolero' some other operation by which we may gain positions of advantage and also directly or indirectly take some of the weight off Russia."

Although American military officers still opposed what they called sideshows, Roosevelt liked the idea of an early commitment in the European theatre of war, particularly since he had promised Foreign Minister Molotov that the Western Allies would take some action in Europe that year. In this context, "Gymnast" seemed attractive.

The loss of Tobruk in June and the British withdrawal to El Alamein reinforced the President's desire, even though Marshall continued to say that "Gymnast" would be indecisive and a heavy drain on the "Bolero" resources.

Furthermore, Marshall said, "Gymnast" would jeopardise the chance of Russian survival and undermine commitments made to the U.S.S.R. "Sledgehammer", he felt, was necessary to keep the Soviet Union in the war.

To gain final agreement on a combined Anglo-American operation in 1942, Roosevelt sent Hopkins, Marshall, and Admiral Ernest J. King, Chief of Naval Operations, to London in July. When the British and Americans found themselves deadlocked – the former favouring North Africa, the latter inclining toward a cross-Channel endeavour – Hopkins cabled Roosevelt for instructions. Late in July, Roosevelt decided for a North African landing, now called Operation "Torch".

An American show

Already the Allies had agreed that an invasion of French North Africa had to be, in appearance, a completely American operation. The French remained bitter about what they considered the less than all-out British contributions, particularly in air forces, to the campaign of 1940. They still resented the British attacks on the French fleet shortly after the French surrender. Although the armistice provisions carried a pledge that the French would fight to repel any invasion of North Africa, they presumably remained essentially anti-German. Given the long ties of Franco-American friendship dating from Lafayette's contribution to the American side in the War of Independence, would the French, who would certainly oppose a British landing, permit American troops to come ashore against only token resistance? The Allies hoped so. But since the Americans lacked the means to invade without the British, "Torch" would have to be a combined invasion. A solution was found in having the initial landing waves consist solely of American soldiers. The commander of the overall operation would also have to be an American.

Since the "Bolero" build-up would have to be diverted, at least in part, to "Torch", Eisenhower became the Allied Commander-in-Chief. He had never been in combat, but he had impressed all his superiors –including Douglas MacArthur, for whom he had worked in the Philippines before the war–with his quick mind, his thorough grasp of military matters, and his ability to make people of different backgrounds work together in harmony. Yet he was an unknown quantity, and "Torch", a complicated venture to be undertaken in considerable haste, would be a serious challenge. As it turned out, he grew in stature and self-confidence as the war progressed, measuring up repeatedly to the increasing demands of his position.

As his Deputy Commander-in-Chief, Eisenhower chose Major-General Mark W. Clark, a hard-driving and energetic infantryman who had been wounded as a young officer in World War I. Just before America entered World War II, Clark had become the right hand man of Lesley J. McNair, who directed the training of the U.S. combat forces. Clark had worked indefatigably to prepare American soldiers for battle. He had then accompanied Eisenhower to England. There he commanded II Corps, which consisted of the U.S. combat forces in the United Kingdom. As Eisenhower's deputy, Clark would prove to be an invaluable help, not only in the planning and execution of "Torch" but also in dealing with the French in North Africa. He would also become a more than competent comman-

der of high rank in his own right.

For his Chief-of-Staff, Eisenhower asked Marshall to make available from Washington Major-General Walter Bedell Smith, a tough and uncompromising organiser, manager, and administrator. He would run Eisenhower's headquarters, known in North Africa as Allied Force Headquarters, with an iron hand, and he would carry out his chief's instructions to the letter so that British and American staff officers worked together on an integrated and Allied, rather than on a separate nationalistic, basis.

As an example of the unity upon which Eisenhower insisted, when an American officer during a heated argument called his counterpart a "British son of a bitch", Eisenhower sent him home to the States. Calling him simply a son of a bitch would have been tolerable.

The original idea of "Torch" was to have two landings, thus requiring two major ground forces, one British, the other American. Lieutenant-General Sir Harold Alexander was initially selected to command the British part, then Lieutenant-General Bernard L. Mont-

△ *American troops load up a truck with jerricans of petrol. Stimson and Marshall both fully realised the importance of a good supply service to a successful advance, and made sure that this received a high priority in the pre-war expansion of the armed forces.*

△ Although not strained to the same extent as Great Britain's, American railways still had to be organised to give first priority to war supplies and to troop movements.

△ By 1945, U.S. war production had far outstripped that of any other combatant, but it was only by careful initial planning, rather than a headlong rush into premature expansion in 1940 and 1941.
▷ Sherman tanks come ashore from a tank landing ship during manoeuvres.

gomery; but when these two were assigned to the Western Desert, Lieutenant-General Kenneth Anderson was given the job. For the American ground force commander, Marshall unhesitatingly chose and Eisenhower enthusiastically accepted Major-General George Patton.

Flamboyant in his personal life style, Patton was a thoroughly professional soldier. Older than Eisenhower and Clark, he had served with Pershing in Mexico and in France. He had become America's foremost tank protagonist in World War I by organising and leading a brigade of light tanks in the St. Mihiel battle and the Meuse-Argonne offensive, where he was wounded. In 1941, he took command of the 2nd Armoured Division, was soon advanced to head I Armoured Corps, and in 1942 was in charge of the Desert Training Centre where infantrymen, tank crew, gunners, and others learned the techniques of battle. Patton was aggressive and experienced in combat, and he would soon become known as America's best fighting leader.

At the end of July, Marshall summoned Patton from the south-western part of the United States to Washington to start planning for "Torch". Early in August, Patton's headquarters, known variously as I Armoured Corps, Provisional Task Force A, and finally Western Task Force, was set up in the War Department directly under Marshall's Operations Division.

Meanwhile, planning had started in London. A Combined Planning Staff of British and American officers, responsible to Eisenhower, worked under Alfred M. Gruenther. Patton flew to London to help and stayed for two weeks, conferring and collaborating with Eisenhower, Clark, and British participants. But hammering out a plan suitable to both nations and responsive to the available resources was extremely difficult.

The aim of "Torch" was to seize Morocco, Algeria, and Tunisia, and the problem of where exactly to land had to be measured against the considerable threats posed by U-boats in the Atlantic and the Mediterranean, enemy aircraft operating from Sicily and southern Italy, possible French opposition, and conceivable Spanish intervention on the side of the Axis.

Although there were no Axis troops in French North Africa, as agreed in the armistice of 1940, the proximity of Tunisia to Sicily made it extremely likely that German and Italian forces would be dispatched to counter Allied landings. To forestall such action, some planners argued that the invasion should take place as far eastward in French North Africa as was reasonably safe. Others felt that landings entirely inside the Mediterranean would be too dangerous because the Strait of Gibraltar might be blocked to Allied shipping. They wished to make at least one landing on the Atlantic coast.

The plan finalised

Not until early September was agreement finally reached that "Torch" would consist of three major landings. The Western Task Force was to be wholly American in composition. Patton would command the ground troops, Vice-Admiral Henry Kent Hewitt, a solid, no-nonsense sailor, the ships. They would sail from Hampton Roads, Virginia, in the Norfolk area, and come ashore near Casablanca in French Morocco.

The Centre Task Force was to consist of American ground troops transported from the United Kingdom in British ships to Oran in Algeria. The ground force commander was Major-General Lloyd R. Fredendall, a rough-talking and blustering man superficially similar to Patton. Fredendall had commanded II Corps in the United States, and when Clark became Eisenhower's deputy, Fredendall flew to London to reassume that command. Several months after "Torch", he would prove incapable of keeping firm control over his troops in the battle of Kasserine Pass in Tunisia, and would be relieved.

The Eastern Task Force was also formed in the United Kingdom. It was to be predominantly British in composition, and was to land near Algiers. As a façade, and therefore making the initial landings, would be a relatively small American force under Major-General Charles W. Ryder, commander of the 34th Division. A competent soldier, he would remain at the head of his division for most of the war.

Following the American landings at Algiers, British troops under Anderson would come ashore in force, as the 1st Army, dash eastward to Tunis, and prevent Axis forces from entering the country.

The mission of all three major task forces was to gain control of French North

Africa, hopefully with French assistance. The Allies had no wish to displace the French presence; instead, they wanted to sustain and enhance French authority over the potentially restless native populations. This would enable the Allies to fulfil their military requirements – rush to Tunis, establish a great supply base, begin to rearm and re-equip the French military forces, which had obsolete weapons – without having to divert troops to guard military installations and to patrol the countryside. The Allies also desired to intimidate Franco's Spain and prevent it from entering the conflict. They expected to forestall an Axis occupation of Tunisia.

A larger strategic result was envisaged by plans to co-ordinate Eisenhower's forces with the British Middle East forces under Alexander. Specifically, the 8th Army under Montgomery was to launch an offensive against Rommel in Egypt shortly before the "Torch" landings. If the British could dislodge Rommel's Italo-German army from El Alamein and send it reeling back across Libya, the "Torch" landings, combined with an 8th Army push into Tunisia, would close the trap on Rommel's forces.

The elimination of these Axis troops would give the Allies complete control over the northern shore of Africa and open the possibility of further operations across the Mediterranean into the European continent.

The U.S. armed forces

But where were sufficient well-trained and well-equipped American troops to be found for "Torch"?

The Regular Army in 1939 had numbered only 145,000 officers and men. They were scattered among 130 posts in the continental United States, mostly in parcels of battalion size. Field army commands hardly existed, and corps area commands were administrative in nature. Nine divisions were authorised, but only three were anywhere near being up to strength; the others were nothing more than brigades.

In November 1939, three months after the outbreak of World War II, Congress authorised an army of 280,000 men. This would bring all nine Regular divisions up to strength and permit the formation of two more corps headquarters and certain other miscellaneous units, groups, and headquarters. Not until May 1940, when the Germans launched their attack on the Low Countries and France, did President Roosevelt request authority to call the National Guard into Federal service and to order individual members of the Organised Reserve Corps to active duty. Late in August, Congress granted that authority, but with the proviso that non-Regular forces could remain in active Federal service for only one year.

By the Selective Service Act, passed in September, Congress authorised an army of 1,400,000 men – a ten-fold increase over the previous year; but again, the conscripted men were to serve for only 12 months. America's geographical isolation had promoted a spiritual isolation, and although Americans were generally sympathetic to Great Britain and France – they were shocked by the collapse of France – public opinion indicated that World War II was none of America's concern.

▽ *A truck is lowered to the waiting harbour personnel from an American ship. With her vast production capacity and great experience of long distance road transport under adverse conditions, America was able to motorise her divisions as no other nation could, and also supply many of the needs of her allies.*

Meanwhile, the rapidly expanding Army created a General Headquarters in July 1940. Marshall, while remaining U.S. Army Chief-of-Staff, became Commanding General; McNair was his chief-of-staff "to direct and support the training of the troops". The new organisation prompted some changes in the methods for teaching soldiers to be effective military men. Formerly, all recruits had received their basic training in the units to which they were assigned. Now, the system was improved by giving individuals military training at General and Specialised Service Schools and by giving key individuals, both enlisted and commissioned, advanced and specialised training in specifically designated small units.

A slow start

Nevertheless, preparation for war proceeded slowly. Not until March 1941 were four American defence commands activated, much in the manner of the British area commands. At the same time several Replacement Training Centres were opened to handle the large influx of citizen soldiers known as selectees or draftees. Designed for mass production, the system provided that new soldiers rotated in cycles through special centres devoted to individual basic and special training. This relieved the field units of responsibility for individual training, allowing them to concentrate on unit exercises, and also made possible a steady flow of partially trained men to tactical units.

Training thus became standardised in the early stages of indoctrination. The result was that the field units could depend on a common foundation among their incoming recruits, who had been trained in combat specialities such as infantrymen, tank crew, gunners, or in administrative specialities such as cooks, clerks, and radio operators. Not long afterwards, ten Officers Candidate Schools were opened.

Yet preparations for war were half-hearted and bumbling, with little sense of urgency, little appreciation of the nature of the war, little thought that, if America became involved, there would be precious little time to get ready for combat. Some of this could be ascribed simply to growing pains and inexperience, for the Army at the end of 1941 consisted of

1,700,000 troops organised into 37 divisions and 67 air combat groups, a sizable increase.

Pearl Harbor swept away all the uncertainty, much of the red tape, and the congressional restriction on keeping men in uniform for only 12 months. A thorough reorganisation, in March 1942, modernised and streamlined the Army. The War Department functioned as before, but immediately below that echelon were created three major commands at home, Army Air Forces, Army Service Forces, and Army Ground Forces. The last, under McNair, was responsible for preparing individuals and units for overseas deployment.

A.G.F. quickly formed a Replacement and School Command, an Armoured Force, a Tank Destroyer Command, an Anti-Aircraft Centre, eight unit training centres, 14 replacement training centres, and seven service schools. By then the authorised strength of the Army had been raised to a goal of 4,500,000 by the end of the year. Similar augmentations affected the Navy and the Marine Corps.

The Army had held a series of great practice manoeuvres in 1941, exercises larger in scope and in the numbers of men involved than had ever been done before in peace-time. These had revealed serious deficiencies in the combat expertise of the units. To remedy the defects, a more systematic schooling of certain

△ *Admiral Jean Darlan, head of the French armed forces at the time of "Torch", and senior member of the Vichy régime in North Africa during the Allied invasion. As deputy premier in 1941, Darlan had been in favour of limited co-operation with Nazi Germany, but with his dismissal from ministerial power in spring 1942 he had veered to the Allied cause. After the Allied landings, he negotiated a cease-fire, which he justified by the subsequent German over-running of Unoccupied France. He was assassinated by a French monarchist on December 24, 1942.*

officers and enlisted men was undertaken. These key persons became cadres or nuclei around which new units were built and trained.

By 1942, the typical training period consisted of 17 weeks for individuals, 13 weeks for units from squad to regiment, and 14 weeks for exercises by the combined arms. Thus, training was progressive. Men proceeded from individual basic and special training to small-unit training, to larger exercises, and finally to manoeuvres involving large forces.

The difficulties of raising, equipping, and training a large military establishment for all the services were enormous. Camps, barracks, installations of all kinds, and training grounds had to be built or enlarged all over the United

△ *Further facets of the American build-up for "Torch": unarmed combat and assault landings under cover of a smokescreen.*

States. Shortages and obsolescence of equipment hampered instructors and students, who were forced to rotate weapons and other *matériel* among various groups and who were compelled to improvise–for example, using broom sticks as rifles. Recently formed units were frequently stripped for cadres to activate other units or to make up shortages in formations assigned overseas. Veteran N.C.O.s and officers who could carry out efficient and effective training programmes were in terribly short supply.

Yet somehow vast numbers of civilians were transformed into military personnel. The essential training philosophy was to make soldiers learn by doing. The emphasis in practices and rehearsals was on realistic battle conditions. So rigorous was the training that many troops finding themselves in combat for the first time

commented, "Hell, this is no worse than manoeuvres."

All sorts of tests were devised to measure the proficiency of individuals and units. When passing grades were attained, the delivery of trained and equipped formations to ports of embarkation culminated the training process. Although most units received additional work overseas before entering combat, theoretically when they were released to port commanders for staging and shipping, they were ready for combat.

Yet chronic shortages of personnel and equipment complicated procedures. Usually when a unit was earmarked for movement, a hurried draft on other organisations for men and *matériel* was necessary. This cycle of robbing certain units to replenish others led to a condition where partially trained and equipped men were often a large component of the formations sent overseas. It also had an adverse effect on the units that had been stripped.

For example, to mount "Torch" General Marshall had to order certain non-participating units to furnish men and equipment in order to fill shortages in the Western Task Force. This reduced eight divisions completing the training cycle to such low levels that six to eight months were required to restore them. There was simply not enough to go around during the swift expansion of the American armed forces.

When the War Department gave notice that certain numbers of various types of units were required overseas, A.G.F., A.A.F., and A.S.F. designated the specific units to perform the final preparations for overseas movement, which became known as "POM". An immense co-ordination to transport men, equipment, and supplies to the port was necessary, and as late as August 1942, McNair wrote to Marshall: "The whole question of staging areas is confused and rather complicated."

Patton's unorthodoxies

Part of the complication for "Torch" came from the impetuous nature of Patton, who often acted independently and disregarded proper channels of liaison and of command. One A.G.F. officer explained the confusion by saying, "Individuals in Washington"–he meant Patton–"have called units direct and have given instructions. There have been times when we didn't know whether they were official, personal, or what."

Another wrote; "Frequent changes of instructions on troop movements have been normal . . . This condition appears to be getting worse . . . The condition was aggravated by the introduction of . . . General Patton's headquarters, here in Washington, which dealt directly with the Desert Training Centre and issued certain instructions at variance with those issued by the office [A.G.F.] without notifying this office . . . In addition to this, the Services of Supply issued directives to its supply agencies to ship equipment direct to the units."

Although the training of the Western Task Force was Patton's responsibility, his units were actually prepared for amphibious warfare while assigned to the Amphibious Force, Atlantic Fleet, which had constructed a training centre during the summer and autumn in the Norfolk area, with schools for commanders and staffs and for various specialists. Army and Navy instructors taught men to serve as transportation quartermasters, as members of shore fire control teams and of beach parties, as boat operators, and the like.

Problems inevitably arose between Patton and the Navy. As Marshall later recalled: "Patton and the Navy were in a scrap all the time. He would get off a wild punch and the Navy would fire up." At one point Admiral King talked to Marshall about replacing Patton with another commander. But Marshall insisted that the qualities that made Patton an outstanding combat leader made him difficult to work with.

Before leaving on the invasion, Patton expressed doubt to Marshall that the Navy would be effective in putting his troops ashore. But two days before the landings, while still at sea, Patton wrote to the Chief-of-Staff:

"I should like to call your attention to the fact that the relations between the Army and Navy in this convoy could not possibly be more satisfactory. Admiral Hewitt and his Chief-of-Staff, Admiral John L. Hall, [have] shown the utmost co-operation and the finest spirit. My doubts have been removed."

Much of the confusion in the Norfolk area attending the preparations and the shipment of Patton's Western Task Force stemmed simply from the fact that it was the largest combat-loaded force, 60,000 men, ever to sail from the United States. Facilities were strained to the utmost. Men were lodged in a variety of camps, posts, and stations along the eastern seaboard, some quite distant from the port of embarkation.

The 1st Infantry Division completed amphibious training in the summer of 1942 and sailed for the United Kingdom to become part of the Centre Task Force. The 9th Infantry Division, less its 39th Regimental Combat Team, which also sailed for England to join the Centre Task Force, moved in and underwent the amphibious training cycle. The 3rd Infantry Division trained on the west coast and arrived at Camp Pickett, Virginia in mid-September. The 2nd Armoured Division rehearsed at Fort Bragg, North Carolina and elsewhere on the east coast.

These formations–the 2nd Armoured and 3rd and 9th Divisions–were the major components of the Western Task Force, and their training was harassed by incessant withdrawal of men for assignment to Officers Candidate Schools or to cadres for new units. The air forces were expanding so swiftly that they could not spare enough aircraft and personnel to train with the ground troops to achieve effective air-ground co-ordination.

Meanwhile, officers were making frantic inspections of combat readiness while others were checking equipment and supplies. Throughout the various preparations for combat, men had to be fed, clothed, cared for medically, and seen through a host of what would otherwise have been routine measures.

△ *Robert Murphy, a senior U.S. official in French North Africa, was largely responsible for the information, both accurate and inaccurate, on which the Americans based their plans.*

△ *American infantry on exercises in wooded terrain.*

CHAPTER 79
TORCH: a two-front war for Rommel
by Martin Blumenson

The whole preliminary period came to an end late in October, as the official historian has written, "in an atmosphere of unrelieved improvisation and haste, an unavoidable consequence of the determination to undertake an operation which stretched resources to the limit".

More than 100 ships transported Patton's men, and this was too large a convoy to go from a single port without attracting attention. They left in small packets at various times from various places, ostensibly bound for different destinations, and then assembled at sea. They were discovered by a U-boat during the crossing, but they managed to get off the shore of Morocco at the designated time. There a high surf, a more or less normal condition in those waters, threatened to end the invasion before it started.

In the United Kingdom, the units comprising the Centre and Eastern Task Forces prepared for "Torch" in similarly exasperating circumstances. The 1st Armoured Division, commanded by

Major-General Orlando Ward, the 1st Infantry Division, headed by Major-General Terry Allen, and the 34th Infantry Division were the major American components, and they had skimpy amphibious training because time was lacking. Nor were there enough ships and boats, even suitable training sites, to provide thorough rehearsals for the forthcoming combat. Armoured formations trained in Northern Ireland while some elements worked in Scotland and much of the staff was involved in planning in London. The infantry had equally frustrating experiences.

It could well be said, as the official historian remarks, that what the Allies were attempting to do was "the best thing possible within the limitations imposed by inexperience, uncertainty, and the shortness of time, rather than trying to turn out a force completely ready".

The assault ships of the Centre and Eastern Task Forces loaded in Liverpool and Glasgow late in September. In accordance with a complex schedule, the ships proceeded to the Firth of Clyde. By October 17, the entire expedition was assembled there. Five days later, the force moved out in a series of small convoys, which proceeded toward Gibraltar. It moved safely through the strait during the night of November 5-6.

Would the French co-operate?

Deep within the Rock of Gibraltar, in damp and restricted quarters, Eisenhower, Clark, and the principal staff members of Allied Force Headquarters—who had flown there from the United Kingdom—listened for news of the impending contest. Eisenhower and Clark also awaited the arrival on November 7 of General Henri Giraud, who was brought secretly by submarine from southern France to discuss whether, and how, Giraud could contribute to the operation.

△ *American troops of the Centre Task Force land in the Gulf of Arzew, near Oran, on November 7. No resistance was met.*
◁ *Men of Patton's Western Task Force clamber down boarding nets from a cruiser to their landing craft.*
Overleaf: U.S. troops wade ashore during the landings in the Gulf of Arzew. The ease of these North African landings unfortunately led to overconfidence, which was to be shattered by the heavy losses of future landings in Sicily and Italy.

In what seemed like interminable conversations, Eisenhower was unable to persuade Giraud to go to North Africa and try to rally the French authorities, who were loyal to the government of Marshal Pétain, over to the Allied side. Giraud would do so only if he received supreme command of the Allied expedition then under way and if he could divert part of it directly to a landing in southern France. This was, of course, hardly practical.

After the invasion Giraud agreed to help. By this time, the Allies were negotiating with Admiral Darlan, Pétain's second in command, who by chance had happened to be in Algiers visiting his sick son in hospital there. Darlan was the highest governmental official on the scene, and he represented the legal authority of France. The Darlan deal, as the arrangements were later called, would prevent a protracted Allied struggle with the French in North Africa. But this could hardly be envisaged as the Allies made ready to assault the coast.

All three task forces were to land simultaneously in order to make the maximum impression on the French. Although the military were sure to offer at least token resistance, some French officers had promised to help the Americans come ashore. These had learned vaguely of the planned invasion from Robert Murphy, an American diplomat stationed in Algiers, and from General Clark who, two weeks before the landings, made a secret and hazardous trip by submarine to a clandestine meeting with sympathisers at Cherchel in Algeria. Unfortunately, security considerations made it impossible to inform the French of the exact time and places of the landings. As a consequence, the assistance that was given so forthrightly was poorly co-ordinated and of small concrete value.

The amphibious forces were to hit the beaches before dawn November 8. Yet each task force commander had discretion to set his exact time because of differing conditions of tide, moonlight, wind, and sunrise at the various sites. The Eastern and Centre Task Forces adopted an H-hour of 0100 hours, Greenwich time; the Western 0400.

The Western Task Force planned to anchor its troop transports several miles offshore, there to release the landing craft already swinging from davits. These boats would assemble alongside the transports to take aboard the troops. Thus loaded, the landing craft would circle nearby until a signal was given for them to form into waves at a line of departure marked by two control vessels. Escorted by guiding vessels equipped with radar and other navigational aids, the landing craft would then proceed on a predetermined schedule toward the shore. There was to be no preliminary shelling, but fire support ships were to take stations from which to shell shore targets if necessary. The waves of landing craft would go in at intervals to allow each wave to unload and pull back from the

▽ *As the invasion got under way, thousands of leaflets like this, claiming that the Americans came as the friends of France, to fight against Germany and Italy, were dropped. Vichy reacted as might have been expected—the landings were to be treated as nothing less than an overt act of war and were to be resisted.*

Message du Président des Etats Unis

Le Président des Etats Unis m'a chargé comme Général Commandant en Chef des Forces Expéditionnaires Américaines de faire parvenir aux peuples de l'Afrique française du Nord le message suivant:

Aucune nation n'est plus intimement liée, tant par l'histoire que par l'amitié profonde, au peuple de France et à ses amis que ne le sont les Etats Unis d'Amérique.

Les Américains luttent actuellement, non seulement pour assurer leur avenir, mais pour restituer les libertés et les principes démocratiques de tous ceux qui ont vécu sous le drapeau tricolore.

Nous venons chez vous pour vous libérer des conquérants qui ne désirent que vous priver à tout jamais de vos droits souverains, de votre droit à la liberté du culte, de votre droit de mener votre train de vie en paix.

Nous venons chez vous uniquement pour anéantir vos ennemis — nous ne voulons pas vous faire de mal.

Nous venons chez vous en vous assurant que nous partirons dès que la menace de l'Allemagne et de l'Italie aura été dissipée.

Je fais appel à votre sens des réalités ainsi qu'à votre idéalisme.

Ne faites rien pour entraver l'accomplissement de ce grand dessein.

Aidez-nous, et l'avènement du jour de la paix universelle sera hâté.

Dwight D. Eisenhower

DWIGHT D. EISENHOWER
Lieutenant Général, Commandant en Chef des Forces Expéditionnaires Américaines.

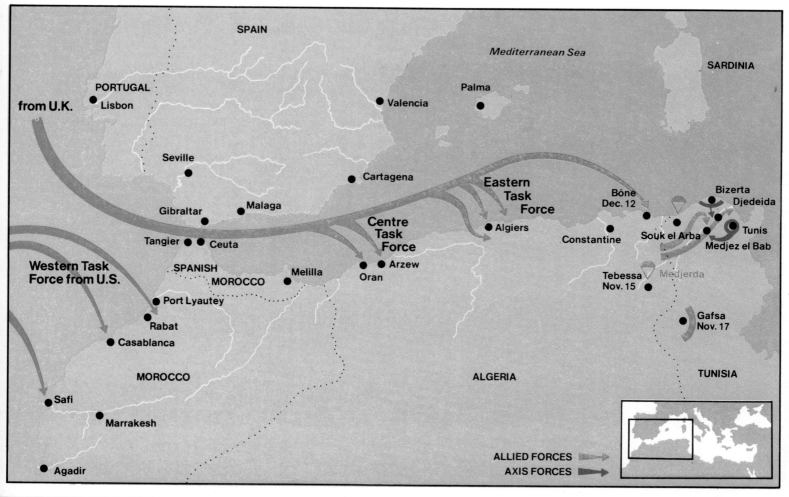

ALLIED FORCES →
AXIS FORCES →

△ The "Torch" landings, bringing together the invasion fleets from the United States and Great Britain for America's first commitment to the European Theatre of Operations and the "Germany first" principle.
◁ American transports wait off Mers el Kébir to land their men.
▽ The Allied hand stretches out greedily to take North Africa's wine, grain, dried vegetables, potatoes, and oil in this somewhat fanciful Vichy poster aimed at the metropolitan French housewife.

NOTRE COMBAT
pour la Nouvelle France Socialiste

Comment ils nous aiment!

△ *American infantry, happy and proud, march to the takeover of Algiers' Maison Blanche aerodrome.*
▷ *Royal Air Force ground crews rest on Maison Blanche aerodrome shortly after the capture of this strategically important area.*

attack groups and took sub-task forces to positions off the beaches of Safi, Fedala, and Mehdia. Although Patton's objective was Casablanca, the city was too strongly fortified and defended to be taken by frontal assault from the sea. He had therefore divided his troops into three landing forces. Those going ashore at Mehdia were to capture the airport at Salé; the other two forces, after establishing beach-heads, were to converge on Casablanca from the landward side.

Up to virtually the last minute, the surf conditions made landings dubious. But when final readings indicated that the weather might moderate, Hewitt decided to gamble and go. Instead of finding a heavy swell, the troops sailed the last few miles to their beaches in almost a flat calm. In a letter to Marshall about a week later, Patton explained why this had happened. "In spite of my unfortunate proficiency in profanity," he wrote, "I have at bottom a strongly religious nature. It is my considered opinion that the success of the operation was largely dependent on what people generally call 'luck', but what I believe to be Divine help."

Major-General Lucien Truscott was in charge at Mehdia, with about 9,000 men from the 2nd Armoured and 9th Divisions. A cavalryman who had accompanied the Canadian troops in the ill-fated Dieppe raid, he showed the competence and dash that would lead him eventually to division, corps, and army command. With his usual proficiency, he took in hand the members of his force, which had become somewhat disorganised in the initial landings at five different points along the shore. French resistance was immediate and strong, and an air bombardment of the ships offshore at dawn of November 8 delayed and reduced the prompt reinforcement and support that had been planned.

At nightfall of D-day, the Americans were in precarious positions. Hard fighting carried them through the second day. Not until the late afternoon of November 10 was the airfield objective taken and secured. As the battle was about to start again on November 11, word came that a cease-fire had been arranged in Algiers.

To obtain the airfield and seaplane base judged to be required for control of the area, Truscott's men had sustained considerable casualties, including 79 killed.

The Safi landings were under Major-General Ernest N. Harmon, a cavalry and

△ △ *Major-General Ernest N. Harmon, who commanded the American forces that landed at Safi, some 6,500 in number.*
△ *Vice-Admiral Henry Kent Hewitt commanded the American naval element in the Western Task Force.*

▽ *Major-General Charles W. Ryder* (left) *led the Eastern Task Force and Major-General Lloyd R. Fredendall the Centre Task Force.*

beach in time to make room for the wave following behind. The first troops to land were to capture the beach and prepare to receive succeeding waves. Later arrivals would reconnoitre inland, expand the beach-head, and penetrate the interior to reach special objectives.

Patton, who had read the Koran during the voyage, issued a circular to his men. "The local population," he said, "will respect strong, quiet men who live up to their promises. Do not boast nor brag, and keep any agreement you make." To his officers he said, "There is not the least doubt but that we are better in all respects than our enemies, but to win, the men must KNOW this. It must be their absolute belief. WE MUST HAVE A SUPERIORITY COMPLEX!"

The Casablanca landings

During the night of November 7, the Western Task Force split into three

tank officer who commanded the 2nd Armoured Division. A bluff and rather rough fellow who was a fighter through and through and who would eventually command a corps, Harmon had a force of about 6,500 men from the 2nd Armoured and 9th Divisions. Their limited training and experience showed at once as they left their transports and moved ashore. There was considerable disorganisation.

On the beaches the Americans met strong opposition from the French. But they fought inland and established a beach-head. On the following day, at Bou Guedra, they met a French force marching from Marrakesh to engage them, and a serious battle ensued. Not until November 10, after blocking the French troops, could Harmon start north toward Casablanca. He took Mazagan on the coast on the morning of November 11 and was starting for Casablanca, 50 miles away, when he learned of the cease-fire.

At Fedala, Major-General Jonathan Anderson, the 3rd Division's commander, headed a force of 16,000 men built around

his division. The same difficulties of getting ashore were encountered, and the same strong French opposition from naval batteries and ground forces was met. The Americans established a beach-head and extended it by heavy fighting, then started toward Casablanca. On the morning of November 11, as they were about to open

◁ *Vichy take-off of an American magazine and a famous U.S. propaganda cry of World War I, "Lafayette, here we come!" The Statue of Liberty and the Stars and Stripes fail to conceal Death reaching out to seize French North Africa.*
△ *A French merchantman capsized at Casablanca.*

1085

◁ *An American White half-track patrols the streets of Casablanca.*
▽ *The scene across Algiers harbour as Allied troops land under cover of a smokescreen on the far side of the bay. With the taking of this city (the major objective of the operation as it was the capital of French North Africa and the nearest of three landings to the final goal of Tunisia) the Allied grip on this major part of Vichy's empire was complete.*

a bombardment of the city as a preliminary for assault, news came of the armistice.

There had been serious fighting at all three landings of Western Task Force, the assumption or the hope that the French were anxiously awaiting their liberation by the Allies proving completely wrong. Patton, a long-time friend of the French, had attempted to negotiate a local armistice throughout the fighting, but his efforts had failed until a general settlement was arranged. After three days of combat in Morocco, American casualties totalled about 550, including 150 killed.

Success at Oran

At Oran, the Centre Task Force, numbering about 22,000 men, was to come ashore in three major operations involving seven different amphibious groups. In general, the 1st Armoured Division, only about half of which was present, was to thrust

inland before daylight and close on the city from the south. The 1st Infantry Division was to encircle the city from the west and east and block the arrival of possible French reinforcements.

The assault convoys found their beacon submarines around 2130 hours on November 7, and sent motor launches to pick up pilot officers. Then the transport groups, preceded by minesweepers, headed for their assembly positions. Landing craft organised themselves into waves and carried men to the beaches of Marsa bou Zedjar, les Andalouses, and the Gulf of Arzew.

The landings were uniformly successful, although the number of troops ashore at the end of the first day was somewhat less than expected. Arzew was captured intact, as was an airfield. The French naval installations and ships at Oran and Mers el Kébir offered weak opposition, and French air efforts were negligible. Only a frontal assault on the Oran harbour, a suicide mission, and an airborne attack on Tafaraoui airfield miscarried.

French forces counter-attacked on the second day, and there was serious fighting. On the third day, an attack on Oran resulted in a sudden armoured penetration into the city. The French authorities surrendered at noon.

△ *A contrast in attitudes: U.S. infantry mop up a damaged battery blockhouse at Fedala while its erstwhile owners display an apparent indifference.*

▽ *The reconciliation starts: a G.I. lights up a cigarette for a French sailor.*

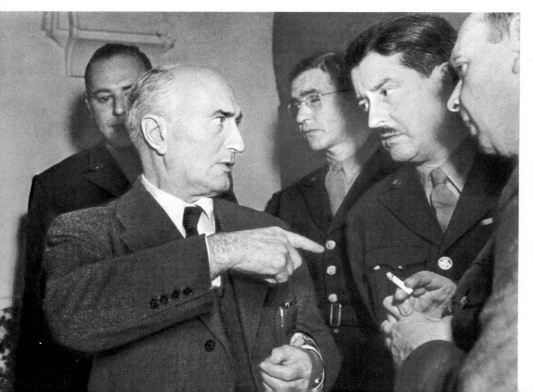

△ Some of the first Americans to land move up through Oran.
▷ An American Stuart light tank, such as was used in North Africa, on manoeuvres.

▽ Admiral Darlan (in civilian clothes) talks to Allied war correspondents after the armistice had come into force.

The seizure of Oran had been accomplished in less than three days by military means alone. This was the only action wholly won by force of arms. Surprise had taken the men ashore without significant French opposition. Sheer determination had carried them inland and to their main objectives rapidly. American casualties totalled about 275 killed, 325 wounded, and 15 missing.

Algiers, the key

Algiers was the most important objective of "Torch" because it was closest to Tunis, the ultimate goal. In addition, the port, railway terminal, two airfields, space for a supply base, city facilities for headquarters, and the fact that Algiers was the seat of government for all of French North Africa made it a great prize.

The Eastern Naval Task Force divided into three columns, one heading for Cape Matifou, two toward Cape Sidi Ferruch. Because there were insufficient Americans for the landings, 7,200 British troops of the 11th Infantry Brigade Group came ashore west of Algiers near Castiglione. The operations went smoothly. French units in the area said they had been instructed not to resist.

Part of the U.S. 34th Division landed closer to the city on its western side. Components were scattered by landing craft along 15 miles of the coast, and all met some French resistance. But the force of 4,350 American and 1,000 British troops took Blida airfield and a small

The French Army started to
serve with the Allies.
△ General Noguès, latterly the
Vichy régime's Resident-General
in Morocco, takes the salute at
a parade of French troops.
▽ French prisoners await their
release after the armistice.
▷ △ The advance into Tunisia:
American paratroopers regroup
after dropping on an airfield
well in advance of the
conventional ground forces.
▷ ▽ Watched by a group of
British soldiers, Americans
heave part of their equipment,
a gun, up a beach.

group entered the city.

The 39th Regimental Combat Team, of
about 5,700 Americans reinforced by 200
British Commandos, landed successfully
east of Algiers and moved to their
assigned positions.

A suicide group of 650 Americans and
several British officers in American uniforms made a direct assault on the harbour. By 0800 hours on November 8, they
had taken their objectives, an electric
power station, a petroleum storage depôt,
a seaplane base, port offices, docks, and
moles. They were then surrounded by

French military units, and had to
surrender.

Meanwhile, Algiers had come briefly
under control of pro-American irregulars
of the French Resistance, who held the
important centres of communication.
They were dispossessed, however, and
French Army units took over.

The presence of Darlan in the city was
fortuitous. Having to decide whether
French North Africa would pass to the
Allies with or without bloodshed, he
radioed Pétain for instructions and received authority to act freely. Around
1600 hours, with Allied troops closing in
on the city, Darlan authorised General
Alphonse Juin to negotiate for an armistice in Algiers, but not for all of French
North Africa. Two and a half hours later,
agreement was reached to halt the
fighting.

On the following day, Clark arrived in
Algiers to negotiate with Darlan a settlement for the rest of North Africa. They
reached agreement late on November 10,
and hostilities between the French and
the Allies ended.

By then, General Anderson had arrived
in Algiers on November 9, and was getting
his 1st Army's movement eastward
organised and started. Tunis, along with
Bizerta, was 380 miles away, and the Axis
nations had already started to pour
troops into the north-eastern corner of
Tunisia by sea and air. French forces
offered no resistance, for officers and men
were anguished by the conflict between
their strong sense of duty to Pétain and
Darlan and by their strong desire to join
the Allies and fight the Axis. While
negotiations took place in Algiers, French
officers waited for instructions on
whether to collaborate with the Axis or
with the Allies. Meanwhile, considerable
numbers of German and Italian troops
arrived through the ports and airfields of
Bizerta and Tunis and established a
strong beach-head. Not until mid-Novem-
ber could French ground troops form a
thin defensive line to keep the Axis units
somewhat bottled up while Anderson's
forces rushed to their aid.

Given the distances, the poor roads,
and the rough terrain, the Eastern Task
Force, predominantly British, made
excellent progress. By November 20,
Anderson's formations were in contact
with Axis units. Five days later, the
British, reinforced by a relatively few
American units known as Blade Force
and by French forces, attacked. But

combat strengths on both sides of the front were equal, and Anderson was at a disadvantage. His line of communications was weak, a depôt system was lacking, and air support was difficult to obtain.

Anderson was not to blame. Allied planners had long been aware that the precipitous advance to Tunis on a shoe-string would be a gamble. Although Anderson tried for another month to crack the enemy defences, increasingly bad weather, including heavy rains, made it obvious that the Allies could not force a favourable decision before the end of the year.

Eisenhower had done all he could to help. He had sent U.S. units from Algiers and Oran, indeed as far away as Morocco, to reinforce Anderson. He had put pressure on the airmen and logistics experts to give Anderson as much support as possible. But on December 24, after visiting Anderson, Eisenhower had to agree that an immediate attempt to capture Bizerta and Tunis would have to be abandoned. A stalemate disappointing to the Allies now set in.

This brought "Torch", the landings and the sweep to the east, to an end. The

△ American paratroopers. Though they managed to capture some strategic points in Tunisia, it took the conventional ground forces some time to move up, and this gave the Axis sufficient time to secure a large bridgehead. To overrun this proved impossible with the limited resources available to the Allies late in 1942.

assassination of Admiral Darlan on the same day, December 24, underscored the conclusion of the operation. A new political situation now had to be dealt with. There were also new military conditions. Rommel's forces had been driven from Egypt and across Libya and were about to enter southern Tunisia.

"Torch" represented the first major British-American combined offensive, and it set the pattern for Allied unity and cohesion in subsequent coalition ventures. Largely improvised, "Torch" was a triumph of planning and execution, for it required an unprecedented effort to build up an American task force in the United States, separated by 3,000 miles from the other two task forces and from Eisenhower's headquarters, then to arrange for the entire force to converge simultaneously on the North African coast.

If "Torch" did not immediately bring American troops into contact with the armed forces of Germany, the last two months of 1942 placed them in proximity to Germans and Italians on the field of battle. That confrontation would take place in 1943, probably earlier than could have been expected if the initial operation had been launched elsewhere. But the quick success that the Americans had enjoyed over the French was unfortunate, for as a result an overconfidence, even an arrogance, arose in the ranks. Many American soldiers came to believe that they were invincible. They had but to appear before the Germans, they thought, to win. The battle of Kasserine Pass in the following year would expose how terribly inexperienced they really were.

The hope of securing a quick cessation of French resistance, not only to facilitate the landings but also to enhance the subsequent operations into Tunisia, had worked. The French had fought bravely despite their outmoded weapons and equipment. Many were wounded, and more than 650 were killed in the fighting. They could with honour enter into the Allied camp and join in the continuing struggle to liberate Europe from the power of Nazi Germany.

Finally, "Torch" was the first of a series of large-scale coalition amphibious landings—Sicily, southern Italy, southern France, Normandy—that would lead the Allies to the final battle with the enemy.

CHAPTER 80
Vichy France falls

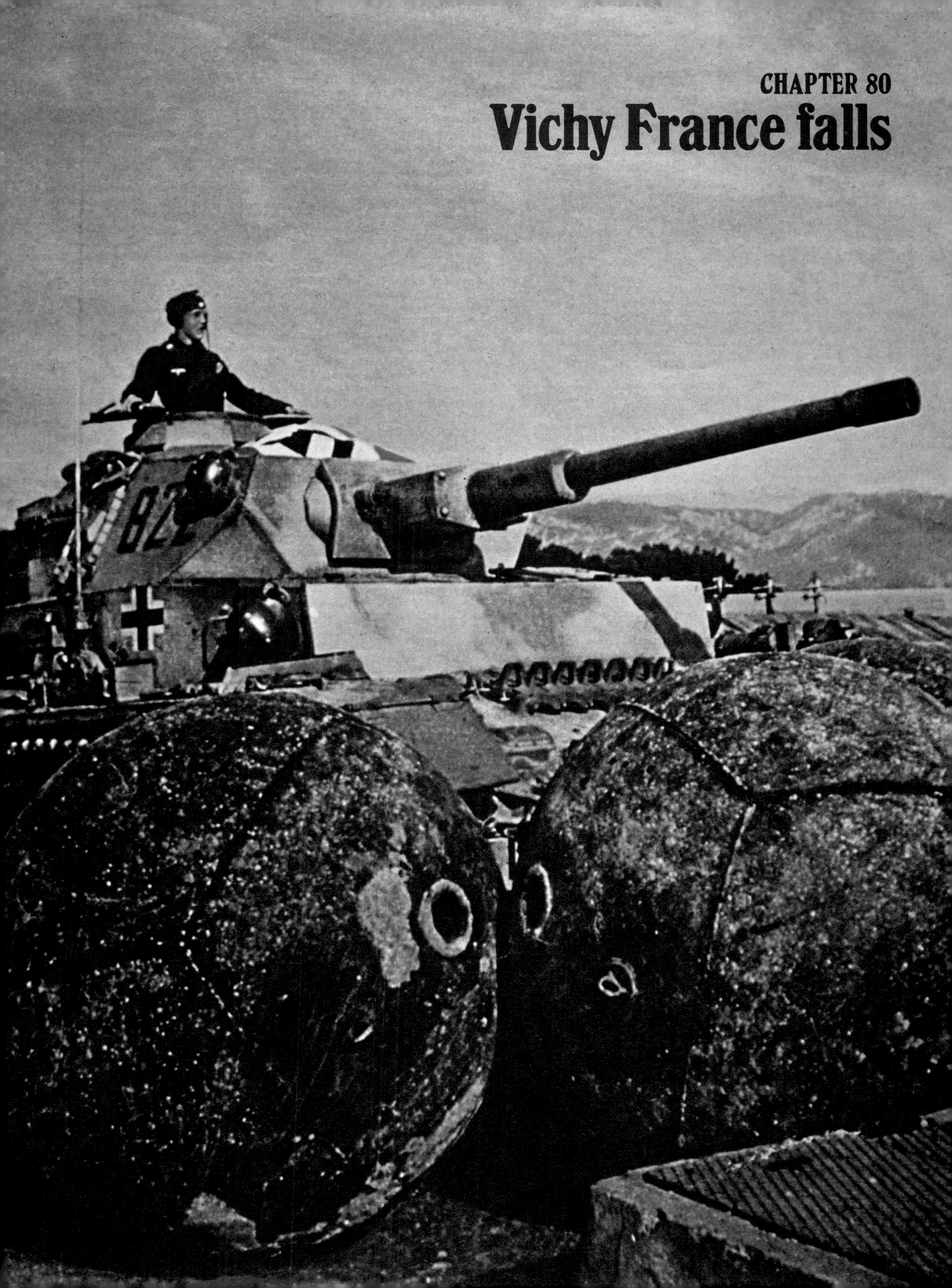

Echoes of the gunfire in North Africa had already reached Vichy when the U.S. *chargé d'affaires* presented himself before Marshal Pétain to read a message from President Roosevelt, announcing the preventive occupation of French North Africa and asking him not to oppose it. Pétain's reply was:

"It is with stupor and sadness that I learned tonight of the aggression of your troops against North Africa.

"I have read your message. You invoke pretexts which nothing justifies . . . France and her honour are at stake. We are attacked; we shall defend ourselves; this is the order I am giving."

In Algiers, however, General Juin cancelled the orders for a counter-attack and proclaimed a cease-fire. This had been agreed with Major-General Charles W. Ryder in the evening of November 8 and he had no difficulty in getting it confirmed by Admiral Darlan, who had come to North Africa to visit his son, who was seriously ill.

On November 9, Generals Clark and Giraud arrived in Algiers, but the latter found that his comrades cold-shouldered him because of his "rebellion". On the following day Darlan nevertheless agreed to a general armistice throughout North Africa and, as requested by General Clark, did so without reference to Vichy. At the same time General Juin notified the troops in Tunisia that the orders to resist "other foreign troops" still stood. This was the end of the fighting between Frenchmen and Americans, which had lasted since the night of November 7–8. According to such statistics as we have been able to find, the French lost a little over 700 killed, about 1,400 wounded, and 400 missing. The 2nd Light Squadron (Rear-Admiral Gervais de Lafond) lost the cruiser *Primauguet* and six destroyers sunk or completely wrecked. Off Oran two other destroyers were lost, one sunk and one driven ashore. Four submarines were also lost, which explains the large number of men missing. The first contacts between General Juin and General Clark were not without their difficulties.

"I confess," Marshal Juin wrote later in his memoirs, "that General Clark, with whom I was subsequently to have such close and friendly relations, especially during the Italian campaign, made a very bad impression on me at this first meeting. This American giant, in his untidy battle-dress, had a hard, secretive look on his face, which was drawn and weary as he had clearly not had any sleep for 48 hours. He always spoke curtly. His badly written note had its own quality of brutal offensiveness. No doubt he was deeply disturbed by the situation he found in Algiers and by the news of the fighting going on in Morocco and around Oran, where the plot to come over to the Allies had not succeeded, and also he probably couldn't make out the respective positions of Darlan and Giraud. He was, in fact, to cable Eisenhower in Gibraltar that night to say that he now had two men on his hands, whereas he had only expected one, and that he didn't know which one he had to deal with."

The Axis riposte

We will not linger over the comedy of errors which followed Marshal Pétain's playing to the gallery as he disavowed Darlan's cease-fire.

On November 11, however, in violation of the Rethondes armistice, the Germans and Italians invaded the unoccupied zone of France. The French Head of State's protests at this act had no practical effect within the country itself, but when broadcast, freed some consciences on the other side of the Mediterranean.

In all this confusion a very important rôle was played by Rear-Admiral Auphan, Minister of Marine at Vichy, and this should be recorded. Through secret channels he managed to let the commander-in-chief of the French forces know that even if Pétain disavowed him with his words he nevertheless approved of his action with his heart. To this effect he had a code which, in defiance of the armistice, had been kept secret from the Germans on June 25, 1940. Thus he cabled Darlan on November 13: "Reference telegram 50803. Complete agreement by Marshal and President Laval but official decision submitted to occupying authorities."

Reorganisation in North Africa

Thereupon agreement was reached in Algiers not only between the Allied command and Admiral Darlan, but between Admiral Darlan and General Giraud, the first assuming the post of High Commissioner in North Africa and the second that of Commander-in-Chief of the French Armed Forces. When he heard this news, the Governor-General, Pierre Boisson, after verifying the authenticity of the telegram quoted above, rallied French West Africa to the Government of Algeria. "This arrangement," wrote Juin, "was communicated to General Clark and Mr. Murphy and was sealed in the afternoon (of November 13, 1942) during the course of a solemn interview with General Eisenhower, the Allied Commander-in-Chief, and Admiral Sir Andrew Cunningham, the only British admiral since Mers el Kébir to find favour with Admiral Darlan for the high qualities of a sailor which he had shown in the Mediterranean and for the way in which he had treated the fleet of Admiral Godfroy when it had taken refuge in Alexandria." As this arrangement could have provoked some astonishment both in London and Washington, General Eisenhower explained it on November 14 to General Marshall in a long telegram, of which we quote essentials:

"November 14.

Completely understand the bewilderment in London and Washington because of the turn that negotiations with French North Africans have taken. Existing French sentiment here does not remotely agree with prior calculations. The following facts are pertinent and it is important that no precipitate action at home upset the equilibrium we have been able to establish.

"The name of Marshal Pétain is something to conjure with here. Everyone attempts to create the impression that he lives and acts under the shadow of the Marshal's figure. Civil governors, military leaders, and naval commanders agree that only one man has an obvious right to assume the Marshal's mantle in North Africa. He is Darlan. Even Giraud, who has been our trusted adviser and staunch friend since early conferences succeeded in bringing him down to earth, recognizes this overriding consideration and has modified his own intentions accordingly.

"The resistance we first met was offered because all ranks believed this to be the Marshal's wish. For this reason Giraud is deemed to have been guilty of at least a touch of insubordination in urging non-resistance to our landing. General Giraud understands and appears to have some sympathy for this universal attitude. All

▽ A German soldier on guard duty in Marseilles after the occupation of Vichy France. In the background is Marseilles Cathedral.

concerned say they are ready to help us provided Darlan tells them to do so, but they are not willing to follow anyone else. Admiral Estéva in Tunis says he will take orders from Darlan. Noguès stopped fighting in Morocco by Darlan's order. Recognition of Darlan's position in this regard cannot be escaped.

"The gist of the agreement is that the French will do what they can to assist us in taking Tunisia. The group will organize for effective co-operation and will begin,

△ *French sailors march off under the eyes of their American captors to a P.O.W. camp.*
▽ *A review of French and U.S. troops in Casablanca late in December 1942. It was the swift transition from the above stage to co-belligerency that prompted the Germans to take over Vichy France to prevent her going over to the Allies.*

under Giraud, reorganization of selected military forces for participation in the war."

On November 12 a British detachment was welcomed with open arms. On the 15th a battalion of American parachutists landed in the region of Tébessa and, on the following day (also dropped by parachute) the vanguard of the 78th Division (Major-General Eveleigh) occupied Souk el Arba in Tunisia, some 90 miles from the capital.

Confused situation in Tunisia

In Tunis Admiral Estéva, the Resident-General, and in Bizerta Rear-Admiral Derrien were both caught between contradictory orders. They had anxiously awaited an Anglo-American landing, but the first troops to arrive on the airport at El Aouïna were German paratroopers in the afternoon of November 9. The situation was all the more delicate in that General Barré, the Supreme Commander in Tunisia, had only 12,000 men under him and that, in accordance with orders dating back to 1941, but still in force, he had to cover the concentration of the Algerian army on the line Béja–Téboursouk–Le Kef in case of invasion by the Axis powers. This line would have afforded him the necessary hilly features to make a stand. In Tunis, however, the Germans and Italians were being reinforced at the rate of 1,000 men a day.

On November 17 Lieutenant-General Walther Nehring, recovered from his wounds sustained at Alam el Halfa, took over command of XC Corps, containing the Axis forces which had landed in Tunisia. At 1100 hours on the 19th he summoned General Barré to clear the way for him into Algeria, and when this was refused he tried in vain to cross the Medjerda at Medjez el Bab. General Anderson drove forward with his 78th

Division, reinforced by a detachment of the British 6th Armoured Division and a group from the 1st American Armoured Division. On November 30 the Allies had established contact with Barre and had advanced to within 12 miles of Tunis.

False optimism

Under these circumstances it is easy to see how Eisenhower optimistically came to announce to Washington the imminent fall of Bizerta. But Nehring was reinforced daily and fighting from his bases, whereas the British V Corps (Lieutenant-General C. W. Allfrey), which had the 78th and the 46th Divisions as well as the armoured units mentioned above, had its communications very stretched. The long guns of the German Pzkw IV and VI Tiger tanks were also making their presence felt. Finally, heavy rains turned the makeshift airfields into lakes and grounded the Anglo-American planes, whereas the Luftwaffe was taking off without difficulty from the tarmac strips at Tunis-El Aouïna and Bizerta. On December 10 the British 1st Army had lost Djedeïda, Mateur, and Tebourba again and with them 1,100 prisoners, 41 guns, and 72 tanks. With these losses went all their hopes of victory before 1943.

The French fleet is scuttled

In France, on November 27, by a fresh violation of undertakings already given, Hitler proceeded to dismember the armistice forces and attempted to seize the fleet which Admiral Laborde had not wished to send out to sea from Toulon when he heard of the German invasion of the occupied zone. The French sailors, carrying out Admiral Darlan's word given to Sir Dudley Pound at the time of the armistice, thereupon scuttled:

    one battleship
    two battle-cruisers
    four heavy cruisers
    three light cruisers
    24 destroyers
    ten submarines
    19 other miscellaneous vessels.

In spite of the surprise, the submarines *Marsouin, Glorieux,* and *Casabianca* succeeded in reaching Algiers, though the *Iris* got herself interned at Carthage. Admiral Darlan did not long survive the fleet which he had done so much to create and train. On December 24, in circumstances which have never been made clear, he was shot by a young fanatic. It can be said of him in justification that he had taken on his new duties with utter dedication and with his usual energy.

△ △ *The end of the splendid French fleet in Toulon: the destroyers* Kersaint *and* Vauquelin, *2,400 tons and five 5.5-inch guns, lie on the bottom in Toulon harbour.*
△ *A detachment of German soldiers watches with stupefaction as major units of the French fleet go up in flames.*

1097

◁ *The blazing form of a French warship in Toulon.*
▽ *The shattered hulk of a Suffren-class heavy cruiser, three of which (Colbert, Foch, and Dupleix) were scuttled on November 27.*

CHAPTER 81

Mussolini in danger

The year 1943 was marked in the Mediterranean by the exploitation of the British victory at El Alamein, the American triumph at Midway, and the Russian recapture of Stalingrad. Not only had the three totalitarian powers failed to achieve their aim of winning the war by 1943, but the reverses that all three of them had suffered obliged them to go on to the defensive and to do this at a time when the American and Soviet colossi were applying the almost inexhaustible resources of their manpower, industry, and other resources to the war effort.

Hitler's blindness

Only in Berlin, or rather in the headquarters at Rastenburg, did anybody in the Tripartite Alliance believe that the war could be won on two fronts. Hitler explained this to Mussolini, via Ribbentrop, on February 25, 1943: the Russians had lost 11,300,000 men while the Wehrmacht had lost only 1,400,000 killed, wounded, and missing. His decision was immutable, Hitler wrote to Mussolini, in a letter which took four hours to read:

"I therefore intend to continue fighting in the East until this colossus finally disintegrates, and to do it with or without allies. For I regard the mere existence of this peril as so monstrous that Europe will know not a moment's peace if, heedlessly balancing on the edge of the abyss, she forgets or simply refuses to face reality . . . I shall fight until the enemy himself admits defeat."

On the question of the British and Americans, Hitler granted that they had "temporarily" achieved certain advantages but, he went on, "what matters is if they succeed in the long run in holding such points by keeping them supplied . . . The continued menacing and obstruction of their sea supply lines is bound sooner or later to lead to catastrophe. I have therefore taken all possible steps to put our U-boat warfare on a virtually indestructible footing."

But in Rome Mussolini did not see the situation in the same light. In his opinion, everything pointed to the British and the

Americans making a major effort in the Mediterranean in order to crush Italy. Thus the thing to do was to transfer south of the Alps the bulk of the Axis forces that Hitler insisted on keeping in the Don steppes. Who knew? Holding Bizerta and Tunis as they did, the Italians and the Germans might be able to inflict a major defeat on General Eisenhower, which would give them French North Africa as far as the Atlantic coast and, in the face of such success, it might reasonably be hoped that General Franco would no longer stand aloof from the joint action which would deny the Allies the Strait of Gibraltar.

The fact remains that this reversal of Axis strategy would have entailed a complete reappraisal of the Third Reich's attitude towards the Soviet Union. Mussolini's health did not permit him to go to Rastenburg where Hitler had summoned him; so he ordered Ciano, in instructions dated December 16, 1942, to put forward the following point of view, when the Führer let him get a word in:

"Mussolini is especially anxious that Hitler should know, as he had already spoken of it to Göring, that he considers it extremely advisable to come to an agreement with Russia, or at least to fix upon a defensive line which could be held by small forces. 1943 will be the year of the Anglo-Saxon effort. Mussolini considers that the Axis must have the greatest number of divisions possible to defend itself in Africa, the Balkans, and perhaps in the West."

Hitler's flat refusal

At the meeting on December 18, 1942, Count Ciano followed his father-in-law's instructions, which also expressed his own point of view. But when he told the Führer that, in the Duce's opinion, the signing of a peace treaty would be an "ideal solution", Hitler repeatedly shouted that when Molotov had visited Berlin in November 1940, he (Hitler) had tried in vain to lead the discussion towards Central Asia but every time he had brought up this idea his guest had mentioned Finland,

△ Hitler and Franco (right) at Hendaye in 1940. Although Franco still refused to join the war on the Axis side, Mussolini and Hitler (especially the former) still had hopes of dragging Spain in on their side, for this would seal the Allies' fate in North Africa.
▷ In the East, Hitler's decision to hold territory at any cost was quickly bleeding the Third Reich white, as this Russian cartoon perceptively points out.

Превращение фрицев

Rumania, Bulgaria, and the Dardanelles. This was perfectly true, in fact, and Hitler's conclusion was:

"The Russia of Stalin still follows the path chosen by Peter the Great for the expansion of his people to the North and South-West. Russia has in no way shown herself prepared to follow the course proposed to her towards India and the Persian Gulf because she regards these aims as secondary. If she were first assured of hegemony over Europe, the rest would follow of its own accord."

Moreover, in his lengthy letter of February 25, Hitler did not restrict himself to repeating to Mussolini that he had no intention of following his advice to make diplomatic soundings in Moscow. He left Mussolini in no doubt that he had also no intention of giving up the Russian campaign which would crush the Soviet giant for ever. Of course, the Axis had to throw back attempts at landings in Corsica, Sardinia, the Peloponnese, Crete, Rhodes, and the Dodecanese, all of which he considered possible in the near future. In other words, what was required was to hold the British and Americans in check while the war in Russia was won.

Mussolini gives in

But what means were available to dispel the threat looming in the Mediterranean? It was quite clear to Mussolini, to the Under-Secretary of State, Bastianini, and to General Ambrosio, who had just replaced Count Ciano at the Foreign Ministry and Marshal Cavallero at *Comando Supremo* respectively, that the offensive mentality which reigned at *Oberkommando der Wehrmacht* would not permit the Germans to deprive the Russian front of the land and air forces which might give the Axis the means for a successful defence of the southern theatre of operations. In fact, the only subject to arise at the conference held in the Palazzo Venezia on February 25–28, in which Ribbentrop, accompanied by General Warlimont, representing O.K.W., explained the Führer's point of view to his Italian hosts, was the military situation in the Balkans and particularly in Croatia and Montenegro.

If, after the evacuation of Tripoli and the destruction of the German 6th Army at Stalingrad, the Duce expected that the

separate herself from the Third Reich, so fast were Italy's means of defence and industrial resources being exhausted. In his diary, Ciano describes the state of depression into which Mussolini had fallen after the Italian defeat in Tripolitania:

"I have seen the Duce again after three days and find him looking worse. But in my humble opinion, what is doing his health more harm than anything else is his uneasiness about the situation. He has rage in his heart over the abandonment of Tripoli, and suffers for it. As usual, he hurled bitter words at the military, who do not make war with the 'fury of a fanatic, but rather with the indifference of the professional'."

He also emphasises the anxiety of the party leaders:

"I have lunch with Bottaï and Farinacci. Both are furious. In speaking of the loss of Libya, Bottaï says: 'After all, it is another goal that has been reached. In 1911 Mussolini uttered his "away with Libya". After thirty-two years he has kept his word.' "

△ *General Vittorio Ambrosio, who succeeded Marshal Ugo Cavallero as Chief-of-Staff at* Comando Supremo *in January 1943, when the latter was dismissed for his activities aimed at preventing a Fascist takeover of the police and army, and the deposition of the King. Ambrosio, who had commanded the Italian 2nd Army in the invasion of Yugoslavia, was soon at loggerheads with the Germans about the policy to be followed in the Balkans.*

Confidence in Japan

▽ *Count Ciano in happier days.*

problem of the war as a whole would be discussed as between equal allies, he must have been terribly disappointed. Having got over the few general questions just mentioned, almost all the rest of the conference was devoted to the support, in any case somewhat limited, that the Italians were giving to General Mihailović and his *Četniks* in the open struggle in which they were engaged against Tito and his Communist partisans. In Hitler's view, there was no difference between them as both were animated by hate for Germany and Italy, and would join the British and Americans if the latter landed on the Yugoslav coast. General Ambrosio, who had commanded the Italian 2nd Army in Croatia, had the temerity to disagree and brought down the rage of the easily-offended Ribbentrop on his head.

And so the Palazzo Venezia conference was characterised by Mussolini's acquiescence in all the opinions that Ribbentrop communicated to him from Hitler. Certainly the Italian dictator, after his illness, was a shadow of his former self, and could not make his voice heard in the argument. But perhaps he realised in his heart that Fascist Italy no longer had the chance to

In Japan, General Tojo, the dictatorial head of the Japanese Government, with the Army united behind him, seems during this same period to have preserved all his confidence in German military might. He was still convinced that the defeat at Moscow and the Stalingrad disaster were only temporary setbacks. Once these were victoriously overcome, the Third Reich would annihilate the last organised forces of the Soviet Union and this would allow the Empire of the Rising Sun to claim its part of the spoils cheaply enough. In particular, the Japanese wanted a foothold at Vladivostok, the northern part of Sakhalin, and Kamchatka.

There was somewhat more caution in the Japanese Foreign Ministry. Before Smetanin, the Soviet Ambassador, returned home on January 1, 1942, Shinegori Togo told him outright and requested him to repeat to Molotov that:

"The present nature of Japanese-Soviet relations in the midst of a world conflict resembles a ray of sunlight shining through a rainstorm; and I hope it will illumine the whole world. If the Soviet Government wishes for peace to be re-established, Japan is ready to offer her-

The changing message from Nazi Germany, according to Soviet propaganda: in 1941 Hitler proudly opens the lid for Goebbels to blare out the glories of the German Blitzkrieg; in 1943 he sits disconsolately as a worn-out Goebbels announces that the war will be a long one as Germany has pulled back and will not be having another Stalingrad.

"The Japanese official concerned pointed out that 'the desire' of the Japanese Navy that Germany should postpone her differences with Soviet Russia, and reach an agreement with the Russians, stemmed from the wish that Germany could then turn all her efforts to destroying British forces in the Far East, and the British position in the Eastern Mediterranean, and in this way and as quickly as possible implement a direct collaboration between the Axis powers and Japan."

Clearly, the result of the Battle of Midway and the operations centred on the island of Guadalcanal could only confirm the Emperor's admirals in their point of view, even more so because the period after which Yamamoto had said that he could no longer guarantee Japanese victory was fast approaching its end.

Though it had been so poorly supported, Togo's initiative had nevertheless provoked the irritation of Ribbentrop. On August 31, he summoned Ambassador Oshima to the *Wilhelmstrasse*:

"The rumour in the world of a separate peace between Germany and Russia has not died down. Unfortunately we have to state that once again it was also Japanese sources which nourished this rumour. It gives strong support to Stalin's propaganda, and he uses it to spur the British to greater efforts. If Japan is using the rumour as cover, to lull the Russians into false security before attacking them, then Ribbentrop has nothing against it. But if not, would Oshima tell his government that 'rumour of a separate peace merely helps our enemy'."

Japanese perseverance

In spite of this outburst, the question came up again a few months later during a conference of Japanese ambassadors to European countries. But in the final analysis, as Oshima told the German Foreign Minister on December 11, if Russia could not make peace on the conditions that Germany laid down, consideration should be given to the situation when "Stalin–having been thoroughly beaten militarily–being finally ready to [make peace] because of the fear of internal revolt, his Japanese government asked to be speedily informed . . . This would be very important to Tokyo as the Army under Yamashita, the conqueror of Singapore, stood on the permanent alert in Manchuria."

self as a mediator and to use all the means at her disposal."

The idea of Japanese mediation between the Soviet Union and the Third Reich was the subject of a discussion at a co-ordination conference held in July 1942 by the principal ministers of Tojo's cabinet and the Army and Naval Chiefs-of-Staff. The following month, Togo instructed the Japanese Ambassador in Moscow, Sato, to sound out Molotov's attitude. However, on September 1, Togo was moved from the Ministry of Foreign Affairs to the Ministry of Greater Asia, and there is reason to suppose that his suggestions regarding Japanese mediation in the Soviet-German war were in some way responsible for this disguised fall from grace.

Ever since the first Soviet winter offensive, the Naval Staff had been thinking along the same lines as the Foreign Ministry. According to a report by the German Ambassador in Tokyo, dated March 14, 1942:

Tokyo abandons hopes of mediation

Ribbentrop seemed satisfied with this clarification, which indicated that Tokyo had given up any attempt at mediation. Furthermore, several weeks later, Tojo proclaimed before the Diet:

"Japan takes an oath to fight to the end, shoulder to shoulder, until a common victory is won, side by side with her German and Italian allies to whom she will give aid and assistance!"

Events would completely belie this foolhardy proclamation later. But, at the moment when the Japanese Army was evacuating Guadalcanal, Rommel was falling back on the Mareth Line, and the defenders of Stalingrad, besieged and starving, were fighting the final battle, should Tojo be accused of deceiving his audience about the coming disaster? Not at all, if account is taken of the unbelievable nonsense that was supplied to him by his Intelligence services concerning losses suffered by the enemies of the Rising Sun during the first year of the Pacific War.

During that year, according to a triumphant communiqué issued in Tokyo on December 7, 1942, 3,798 British, Dutch, and American planes had been shot down or damaged. This was obviously a grossly exaggerated figure, if the air weakness of the three victims of Japanese aggression is considered. The 1947 edition of the *Annuaire de Flottes de Combat*, scrupulously compiled by Henri Le Masson, lists Japanese exaggerations about Allied naval losses as follows:

	Communiqué	Real losses
Battleships	11	4
Aircraft-carriers	11	5
Cruisers	46	14
Destroyers	48	35
Submarines	91	11
	207	69

From this it can be concluded that, though General Tojo could not be completely excused, as often happens he was the victim of his own propaganda.

The German defeats on the Eastern Front at the end of the autumn of 1942, followed by the near annihilation of the Hungarian 2nd Army near Voronezh in January 1943, had been followed by deep disappointment and heart-searching in government circles in Bucharest as well as in Budapest.

Rumania appeals to Mussolini

The defeat of the Rumanian 3rd Army on the Don had already given rise, on November 25, to a heated exchange about the responsibilities for this setback between General Steflea, Chief-of-Staff to Marshal Antonescu, and General Hauffe, leader of the German military mission to the Rumanian Army. At the beginning of January, Hitler demanded the raising of 19 new Rumanian divisions. Consequently, Mihaï Antonescu, the *Conducator*'s nephew and Foreign Minister, summoned Bova-Scoppa, the Italian Ambassador, and asked him to convey a memorandum to Count Ciano in which he revealed the serious fears he felt concerning the future development of the political and military situation. In his opinion, as his uncle and he himself had verified in their recent visit

△ △ General Oshima in conversation with Ribbentrop at Rastenburg. The latter was particularly worried lest Japanese offers of mediation lead to an impression that Germany was weakening.
△ Count Shinegori Togo.

state of affairs in the Mediterranean and the Balkans will deteriorate. My conviction is that England and America have no interest in letting the Russians into Europe and I have precise information to that effect. The Turkish Ambassador came specially to tell me that America and particularly England were pressing on into Europe in order to bring the war to an end, but that they wished at all costs to avoid the collapse of the European system in favour of Russia. I have received similar reports from Portugal."

For all this, Mihaï Antonescu did not reach any positive conclusion. But since Germany, obsessed by her own problems, had no interest in thinking about the future of Europe, Italy became the only country Rumania could call on, and this made Antonescu decide: "Ask Count Ciano to inform me of the Italian point of view through you, if I cannot manage to see him".

On January 19, Bova-Scoppa carried out the mission with which he had been entrusted, receiving a most friendly welcome from Count Ciano. On the same day, the Italian Foreign Minister noted in his diary:

"The latter [Antonescu] was very explicit about the tragic condition of Germany and foresees the need for Rumania and Italy to make contact with the Allies in order to establish a defence against the bolshevization of Europe."

But Mussolini received his son-in-law's suggestions coldly and confirmed in the clearest terms that he had made his mind up to march to final victory shoulder to shoulder with the Third Reich.

Bulgarian-Rumanian alignment

However, on January 29, a long handwritten report from Filippo Anfuso, Ciano's ex-Principal Private Secretary and now Italian Ambassador in Budapest, revealed that the Hungarian leaders were thinking along the same lines as Mihaï Antonescu: "'We are told,'" Admiral Horthy, Regent of Hungary, had informed him, "that we are a German satellite. Very well. But if Germany cannot defend us against the Slavs, what will become of us?... I still believe that a common Italo-Rumanian front against the Germano-Slav waves would be a sure guarantee of safety for us. We shall continue to fight,

to O.K.W., Hitler appeared obsessed by the Soviet problem. In order to preserve the eastern border of Fortress Europe, he was ready to hurl the flower of European youth into the furnace. When Antonescu had asked Ribbentrop for his opinion on "the immense moral and political problems posed in Europe", the latter had replied that he could give no opinion until Russia had been defeated and added: "Europe must hold. That is the main point."

This blind obstinacy evoked these observations from the Rumanian Foreign Minister:

"Under these circumstances I think that one should assist the German leaders to clarify the situation. If the position in the East gets still worse, Hitler will send all his reserves to that Front, and then the but we live in a state of tension . . .' "

And Nicholas de Kallay, the Hungarian Prime Minister, went even further than Horthy. In the midst of the Flood, the politicians of Hungary crowded round the portholes of their Noah's Ark and tried to see land, asking themselves: "What is Italy doing?" Kallay wrote:

"In these questions . . . lies the naturally understandable anxiety of those who asked themselves whether the Slavs of the South and North will not slaughter the ten or twelve million Magyars before any English, American, Italian, or German military police arrive to save them. In order to imagine this panic state of affairs, it is sufficient to reflect on what has happened recently: the bulls of the Danube and the dogs and cats of the Carpathian plain—in other words the Hungarians and the Rumanians—have decided to negotiate with each other again, though they realize that they are neither Germans nor Slavs, and fear to be devoured by them."

In the end, just like his enemy Mihaï Antonescu, he appealed to Count Ciano, whose friendship the Hungarians had been able to appreciate at the time of the Belvedere arbitration.

Anglo-Hungarian accord

If truth be told, the news of the rapprochement of Hungary and Rumania was not exactly a surprise for the Italian Foreign Minister, as Ambassador Bova-Scoppa had already informed him of it on January 10. On the other hand, a plan of Kallay's and the commentary on it by Anfuso in his "intelligent and clearsighted letter" seemed to have disturbed him more. On January 29 he noted:

"There are no actual facts as yet, but many indications lead one to believe that Hungary has already had some contact with the Anglo-Saxons. Besides, Mariassy [Hungarian ambassador] asked d'Aieta [Ciano's Chief of Cabinet] with a good deal of anxiety if it were true that the Rumanians had been negotiating with the British and that conversations were under way in Lisbon. D'Aieta denied this, but, in reality, what do we do about it?"

In fact, Admiral Horthy's memoirs reveal what Ciano could only suppose in 1943. First contact was made with the British by the Budapest Government in summer 1943 and the two governments reached, doubtless in autumn 1943, a secret agreement, according to whose

terms Allied aircraft flying over Hungary would not be attacked and, in their turn, would not engage in any hostile act against the territory of the Kingdom of Hungary. Then the talks led by Kallay on the Hungarian side turned to the heart of the problem. Horthy writes:

"Between Kallay and myself there was a tacit agreement that granted him (without informing me of every detail) the necessary freedom to take initiatives which, though apparently maintaining normal relations with Nazi Germany, would strengthen our friendship with the Anglo-Saxons, and yet not help the Soviets. It was a delicate task, made particularly difficult, if not impossible, by Roosevelt's policy towards Stalin."

Actually Hitler knew what to expect from Kallay, and Admiral Horthy realised this during his visit to Hitler in April 1943. At that time Hitler was staying at Klessheim:

"He was more than usually irritable," Horthy writes in his memoirs. "My visit had been preceded by Mussolini's. The Italian leader had been accompanied by Ciano's successor, Secretary of State Bastianini, and by the Rumanian Marshal Antonescu. They had all stated they were in favour of negotiating peace. Mussolini, after the now inevitable defeat in North Africa, feared an invasion of Sicily and wanted an agreement with Stalin, while Antonescu, who wanted to make a grand union of all forces to stem the tide from the East, had come out in favour of an agreement with the Western Allies. This 'defeatism', to use the term preferred by the Nazis, shown by two men for whom he felt

◁△ *Another Russian comment: Mussolini, with the dead weight of Hitler's aid around his neck, drowns in the Mediterranean while Hitler has his hand trapped in the "rainbow" of Kursk (a reference to the bow-shaped salient there).*
◁▽ *Mihaï Antonescu, the Rumanian Foreign Minister. Disturbed by the course of events, he too was seeking a way out.*
△ *Filippo Anfuso, the Italian Ambassador in Hungary.*
▽ *A T-34 knocked out at Voronezh. But in this city the Germans and Hungarians suffered a morale-shattering defeat.*

△ *Giuseppe Bottaï, who joined the anti-Mussolini faction after being ousted from his position as Minister of Education.*

▽ *Ivanoë Bonomi, a Prime Minister of the Liberal era who rallied to Ciano's cause after seeing the dangers into which Mussolini's policies had led Italy.*

particular respect, had greatly irritated Hitler and this had not disappeared by the time I arrived and contributed to the way in which I was received. Even Goebbels, who in his heart of hearts was most evilly disposed towards Hungary and myself, noted in his diary that 'Hitler had treated Horthy too severely'."

Ciano's fears . . .

The Italian Foreign Minister was not at all indignant at the news which his representatives in Budapest had conveyed to him, with the usual diplomatic reserve, concerning the possible contact made by Hungarian leaders with the British and Americans. The fact was that since El Alamein, Algiers, and Stalingrad, Ciano had seen the defeat of the Axis clearly written on the wall. Besides, since Hitler obstinately refused to cut his losses, that is to negotiate with the Soviet Union as Mussolini advised him, Ciano saw Italy defenceless or almost so in face of the British and the Americans; already the bombing of Genoa, Milan, and Turin, which had accompanied Montgomery's African offensive, was giving him a foretaste of what 1943 could be like. But Ciano, the son of Admiral Costanzo Ciano, Count of Cortellazzo, scion of a famed and wealthy family of Leghorn, did not feel any of that violent hatred and scorn for the "capitalist" states of Great Britain and the United States, that his father-in-law Mussolini, the ex-schoolmaster and revolutionary agitator from Forlì, had only just recently proclaimed to the Chamber of Deputies once again. Thus one may well believe that Mussolini and his Foreign Minister did not see the situation from the same viewpoint.

. . . and designs

Mussolini's African and Atlantic ambitions made him quite naturally consider Britain, and after her, America, as his main enemy while Ciano, concerned with maintaining Italian influence in the Danube basin and the Balkans, saw danger in the unexpected expansion of Soviet power.

Thus it was that he conceived the idea of replacing the North–South (or Berlin–Rome) Axis, from which he could expect

nothing more, given Hitler's incurable blindness, with a new one, running East–West (Bucharest–Lisbon) which Rumania, Hungary, Croatia, Italy, France, Spain, and Portugal would be invited to join.

In that way a line of neutral, mainly Latin and Catholic powers, would be formed. Here it seems very likely that Count Ciano shared the opinion or the dream of his Rumanian colleague, that the American President and the British Prime Minister would not look favourably on the establishment of "Bolshevism" in Central Europe. Contrary to his father-in-law, he now thought the moment had come to seek a reconciliation with the United States and Great Britain.

Ciano's plans secret no more

Even today there is still some obscurity about the feelers put out by Ciano to try to execute his plan; his famous diary does not mention them at all and, as may well be imagined, he did not use the normal diplomatic channels. It is thought that there were talks in Lisbon soon after El Alamein and in Berne some weeks later.

What is known for sure is that the secret services of the Third Reich managed to obtain some information about the web that Ciano was trying to spin behind Mussolini's back. According to information given in the early 1960's to the British historian F. W. Deakin by Mr. Allen Dulles, at the time Head of United States "Strategic Services" in Switzerland, the cryptographers of the *Abwehr* had managed to break the code which the United States legation in Berne was using at the time; and a dispatch from their transmitter in January 1943 had reported that an anti-German faction was in existence in Rome, with Marshal Badoglio, Ciano, and Count Dino Grandi as its leaders.

Is this statement reliable? It seems so, for at the same time, the late Nicholas Lahovary, Rumanian Minister in Switzerland and himself a great supporter of the "neutral front" was relieved of his post by Marshal Antonescu on the express orders of Hitler and Ribbentrop.

This would explain why, on February 5, Mussolini, who had received, with Hitler's compliments, a copy of the American cable, "changed guard" as he called it and reshuffled his ministers, excluding from his new government those who

◁ *Nicholas de Kallay, Prime Minister of Hungary, talks with Hitler in the gloomy grounds of the latter's headquarters at Rastenburg.*
△ *Propaganda that no longer carried even the slight force it had originally: "They give their blood. Give your labour to save Europe from Bolshevism." But volunteers were minimal – forced labour was to be the order of the day henceforward.*

supported Italy's quitting the war.

"What would you like to do now?" the Duce asked his son-in-law when he received him in his office in the Palazzo Venezia. The latter later noted:

"Among the many personal solutions that he offers me I decisively reject the governorship of Albania, where I would be going as the executioner and hangman of those people to whom I had promised brotherhood and equality. I choose to be Ambassador to the Holy See. It is a place of rest that may, moreover, hold many possibilities for the future. And the future, never so much as to-day, is in the hands of God."

Fearing – as in fact happened – that Mussolini might go back on his offer, Ciano requested the *placet* of the Vatican that same day and immediately received it. This was only to be expected, for Pope

Pius XII's Under-Secretary of State, Monsignor Montini (today Pope Paul VI) seems to have known of his plan to take Italy out of the war. For the same reason, King Victor Emmanuel III said he was "very happy" at the appointment, and the Duke of Acquarone, Minister of the Royal Household, was "delighted".

Count Ciano describes his last interview with the Duce before taking up his new duties in the Vatican:

"He thanks me for what I have done and rapidly enumerates my most important services. 'If they had given us three years longer we might have beeen able to wage war under different conditions, or perhaps it would not have been at all necessary to wage it.' 'Yes,' I answered. 'I have them all in order, and remember, when hard times come – because it is now certain that hard times will come – I can document all

continued on Page 1118

△ *Germany needed not only industrial workers from the countries she had conquered, but soldiers too, as indicated by this poster for volunteers for a Wehrmacht infantry unit.*

1109

MUSSOLINI
A Dictator's Story

Benito Mussolini, *Il Duce,* the self-styled modern Caesar, was a mass of paradoxes. He started life as an archetypal student left-winger only to seize supreme power in Italy at the head of a party which gave the 20th Century one of its most misused words: Fascism. He set the pattern for modern-day European dictatorship and was for years the most admired political figure in Europe, until Hitler arrived on the scene and stole his thunder. In his early days the Nazi leader cut a very dowdy figure beside the splendidly-uniformed Italian dictator – but by 1939 there was no doubt as to which of them was the dominant leader. Mussolini, without whose acquiescence Hitler would never have been able to get away with the Austrian *Anschluss* or the seizure of the Sudetenland, was reduced to asking Hitler nervously not to get Italy involved in a war for which she was not ready.

In the following year – like a teenager robbing a shop to show that he is just as tough as the rest of them – Mussolini took Italy to war, hoping for cheap victories with which to emulate Hitler's military triumphs in Poland, Scandinavia, and the West. The immediate string of disastrous Italian defeats which followed necessitated the sending of German military aid, and Italy was confirmed in her position as Germany's poor relative. Not only

that: Italy was singled out by the Allies as the first of the three Axis powers to be defeated, and that defeat caused Mussolini's fall from power. Although snatched from Allied hands by German airborne commandos and retained as head of a titular Fascist régime, Mussolini remained a pathetic figure for the last few months of his life. And the ultimate humiliation came after he was gunned down by Italian partisans. The people over whom Mussolini had once held supreme power strung up his decomposing body by the heels for the execration of the Milanese mob.

Mussolini was born on July 29, 1883, at Dovia in Forlì province. As a youth he became deeply concerned with the Italian revolutionary movement, and went to Switzerland in hopes of evading military service in Italy. There he devoted himself to revolutionary propaganda until the Swiss authorities lost patience and expelled him; he returned to Italy and performed his military service, afterwards becoming an active member of the socialist movement.

By 1909 Mussolini was in Austrian-occupied Trento, working on the staff of Italian socialist papers. There he associated with Cesare Battisti, a leading Italian nationalist agitator in the irredentist movement, which pressed for the recovery of native Italian territories which had remained under Austrian rule after the unification of Italy in the previous century. Expelled from Austrian territory for his activities, Mussolini returned to Forlì and became secretary to the Forlì section of the Socialist Party. He opposed the invasion of Libya as an imperialist act and got five

1. *Mussolini as a revolutionary in Italy, 1904.*
2. *Corporal Mussolini of the Bersaglieri in 1917, aged 34, before his grenade wound.*
3. *The Mussolini family poses for a group photograph. His daughter Edda married Galeazzo Ciano, making the Duce's foreign minister his son-in-law.*
4. *Two peasant children dance for the Duce during a visit to a farming community.*
5. *Roses all the way for a genial Mussolini, greeted at Lucca by a group of girls in medieval costume.*
6. *A bandaged nose was the only damage inflicted on Mussolini in an attempt on his life in 1926.*
7. *The constitutional front of a budding dictator. This was how Mussolini looked when he became premier in 1922.*

8. *As with the Nazi Party in Germany, the regimentation of youth was an integral part of the Fascist programme. Here Mussolini is awarding prizes in Rome to the winners of a students' sports championship.*
9. *The Duce in action, delivering an impassioned speech in Rome. Balcony harangues became his speciality.*
10. *An incongruous guard of honour: Mussolini gives the Fascist salute to a group of tennis champions and prominent players.*
11. *A recruiting speech to keep the Fascist Militia up to strength. In this speech the Duce appealed for 90,000 volunteers.*
12. *Mussolini plays host in Rome to Göring.*

13

months' imprisonment for inciting the workers of Forlì to resist the war. In December 1912 he became editor of *Avanti*, the official party paper, and became famed for his outspoken editorials. He added to his laurels by supporting the working-class riots of "Red Week" in June 1914–but the outbreak of World War I led to his break with the socialist movement.

Mussolini's initial reaction to the war was to advocate neutrality but he changed his tune and began pressing for intervention, on the grounds that war would favour revolution and that "the proletariat would have better opportunities to develop its class consciousness". He was expelled from the Socialist Party; Italy finally declared war on Austria in May 1915, and Mussolini got his call-up orders in September of that year.

Mussolini served with the crack *Bersaglieri* until he was badly wounded by an exploding grenade in February 1917. Quitting the army, Mussolini reverted to the role of outspoken newspaper editor with the *Popolo d'Italia*, lambasting the pacifist Socialists. And then, on March 23, 1919, he founded the *Fasci di Combattimento* in Milan–the birth of the Italian Fascist movement.

Its motivation was national socialism, and like the Nazi Party in Germany the *Fasci* got considerable support from ex-servicemen who were embittered by peace-time conditions. There was also the encouragement of vested interest, fearful of the possibility of a Bolshevik revolution. But Mussolini got little backing from

13. *Partner of the Axis. Hitler greets Italian officers at a meeting between the two dictators.*
14. *On the Führer's right hand: Mussolini walks beside Hitler at Munich in 1938, when he helped ensure Hitler's takeover of the Czech Sudetenland by intervening on his behalf.*
15. *Lord Halifax and Neville Chamberlain visit Rome in January 1939 on their abortive "good-will" visit. English residents broke into "For he's a jolly good fellow." "What is this little song?" asked the Duce.*
16. *Inspecting a contingent of Italian troops bound for the Eastern Front.*

15

17. *Mussolini is shown a new wireless transmitter intended for use in the Italian army.*
18. *Inspecting the air force.*
19. *A rousing harangue to troops back from service in the Spanish Civil War.*
20. *Hitler and Mussolini in Rome, after paying their respects before the tomb of the Unknown Soldier.*
21. *A cartoon of the Duce—characteristically savage in its execution—by Kukrinitsky of Russia.*
22. *Mussolini makes a speech during a visit to Hitler's H.Q. in Russia.*

the trade unions, and he failed badly as Fascist candidate for Milan in the 1919 elections.

Fascism got its big chance with the widespread workers' demonstrations of autumn 1920. Although the Liberal Government weathered the storm, Mussolini decided to exploit the fears of the moneyed classes by organising armed squads to destroy socialist organisations. The movement grew far more quickly than Hitler's Nazi Party. Mussolini and 35 other Fascists were elected to Parliament in May 1921. In 1922 Fascist groups broke up an attempt at a national strike by the trade unions and socialists, and in October of that year Mussolini's supporters made their notorious "March on Rome". The armed Fascist groups concentrated at Naples and moved on Rome—without Mussolini, who was in Milan. King Victor Emmanuel III refused to support the government's wish to proclaim a state of emergency—and gave Mussolini the task of forming a new cabinet.

Mussolini acted with circumspection. His first cabinet included a majority of non-Fascists, and he was helped out of all measure by the rivalries between the other political parties. Thus he had no trouble in concentrating power in his own hands, being Prime Minister, Minister of the Interior, and Minister of Foreign Affairs, as well as Minister for the Army, Navy, and Air Force. In January 1923 he created the Fascist Grand Council, with members nominated by himself.

in February he converted the **22** Fascist armed squads into a private army by proclaiming the national security militia—the *Milizia Volontaria per la Sicurezza Nazionale.* In the 1924 elections the Fascists secured 65 per cent of the recorded votes.

The Fascist Party was shaken by the storm of indignation which blew up over the murder of the socialist deputy Giacomo Matteotti in June 1924, but—as Hitler was to find in Germany—the opposition parties played into Mussolini's hands by falling back on passive resistance. On January 3, 1925, he took the plunge and announced that he would assume full dictatorial powers. Opposition parties and journals·were suppressed. The Fascist dictatorship had begun.

It was bedevilled from the start by Mussolini's insistence on concentrating all power in the hands of the régime, and as far as possible in his own hands. The economic reforms he put through had a superficial flashiness but were damaging to the country in the long run. Certainly his most genuine achievement was the Lateran Treaty and Concordat with the Papacy in 1929, establishing the present Vatican City state.

From the shrewdness and flexibility of his early days Mussolini grew into a vain, strutting megalomaniac. *"Mussolini ha sempre ragione"*—"Mussolini is always right"—was a key slogan of his régime. But in Adolf Hitler the vainglorious Duce met his Waterloo.

▷ *An added spur for the anti-war faction in Italy was the beginning of heavy bombing raids by the Royal Air Force and U.S. Army Air Forces operating from North Africa.*

▷ △ *Giuseppe Bastianini, who succeeded Ciano at the Foreign Ministry with the much reduced status of Under-Secretary of State, Mussolini adding this portfolio to the excessive number he already held.*
▷ ▷ *Count Dino Grandi, one of the principal leaders of the conspiracy against Mussolini. Grandi had the additional advantage of having the ear of the King.*
▷ ▽ *Marshal Pietro Badoglio, Chief-of-Staff of* Comando Supremo *until December 1940, and now the conspirators' hope as a replacement for Mussolini.*

△ *Monsignor Giovanni Battista Montini, now Pope Paul VI, was at the time Under secretary of State to Pope Pius XII.*

continued from Page 1109

the treacheries perpetrated against us by the Germans, one after another, from the preparation for the conflict to the war on Russia, communicated to us when their troops had already crossed the frontier."

Ciano's successor, Giuseppe Bastianini, was reduced to the status of Under-Secretary of State in the Foreign Ministry. He had been out of touch with diplomacy, the last important position he had held being Ambassador to Great Britain, which he had been up to June 10, 1940. All things considered, therefore, he imagined that his new appointment was intended to allow him to prepare discreetly for Italy's withdrawal from the war, a war which he had spoken against from the beginning. But as he pushed open the door in the Palazzo Venezia on February 10, 1943, he might well have read Dante's line "Abandon hope, all ye who enter here."

For at the first word he mentioned on the subject to the Italian dictator, the latter replied quite sharply:

"It seems to me that you are making a mistake; my intentions are not those which you imagine. We are at war. I am the Foreign Minister. You have specific duties to carry out, but the direction of foreign affairs is in my hands, and my conception is very simple; when one is at war, one stays with one's ally until the end."

However, the Duce had not only taken over the Foreign Ministry but had also kept control of the portfolios of the Interior, War, the Navy, and the Air Force. To these administrative responsibilities must be added the burden of the *Comando Supremo* and the leadership of the Fascist Party. Clearly even the fittest man would have found it difficult to fulfil so many obligations satisfactorily. Then the stomach ulcer which he had thought healed at the end of December flared up again under the influence, it appears, of the bad news which flowed in endlessly from North Africa and the Russian front. So the despotic power which he had taken on himself was equalled only by his inability to exercise it efficiently.

One further remark concerning Mussolini's declaration: the Duc de Saint-Simon once wrote that one of King Victor Emmanuel III's ancestors, the Duke of Savoy, could never be found on the same side at the end of a war as when it had been declared, unless he had changed camps twice. In contrast, the Duce considered that he had to respect the conditions of the Pact of Steel to the letter, because it concerned his personal honour, that of the Fascist Party, and of his country. His partner, on the other hand, had brazenly violated it twice, first by attacking Poland on September 1, 1939 and then by invading the Soviet Union on June 22, 1941, without having consulted his ally. "Nobody is obliged to sacrifice himself on the altar of an alliance," stated Prince Bismarck in a similar situation.

The King steps in . . .

These were the arguments advanced by the exhausted Italian ministers on February 5, 1943, when faced by Hitler's obstinate determination to persevere with war on two fronts. One of those men, Dino Grandi, leaving the Palace on February 12, 1943, after the audience traditionally granted to resigning ministers, said to the King's senior aide-de-camp, General Puntoni:

"One must not have any illusions. Italy should attempt little by little to unhitch her wagon from that of Germany to make the crash less painful. I have always been a supporter of a policy of understanding with Great Britain, and within the limits of my power have always sought to oppose the thrust in the direction of Germany...On the home front, in face of the apathy of the great mass of the people, a general lack of confidence in their leaders, there is resentment of many of the old Fascist elements, who have been frustrated in this desire to make and serve the country. For them, Fascism should be an instrument of redemption. At any moment, in the face of military disaster, a political movement could take shape with a social basis which the Communists would at once exploit. Only the King at the right moment could restore things to their place. It would, however, be a most difficult and dangerous operation. For my part, I am with the King."

Puntoni naturally passed on the offer of service to the King, who replied by conferring on Grandi, as President of the Fascist Chamber, the Collar of the Annunziata, the highest decoration in the gift of the House of Savoy and which, very usefully, gave its holder free access to the Quirinal Palace. Thus the distinction constituted an encouragement to Grandi and furnished him with the means of continuing his talks with the King.

In fact, as the King said in a letter to the Duke of Acquarone, since January 1943 he had "definitely decided to end the Fascist régime and dismiss Mussolini". He was being insistently urged to do so by the old Marshals Badoglio and Cavaglia and by the young Generals Carboni and Castellano. Nevertheless the monarch countered these demands by arguing that a military *coup d'état* would allow the Duce to hide behind the ramparts of the constitution and to mobilise the paramilitary forces of the Fascist militia. In this case, there would be civil war, and everything pointed to Germany's siding with Mussolini, the only man in Italy that Hitler trusted.

. . . and decides to remove Mussolini

On the other hand, if the opposition within the Fascist Party itself could be stirred up, Mussolini would gradually find himself in a minority among his own supporters. This change of heart would bring on a political crisis to which the monarch and, if it became necessary, the Army would find a solution which could be seen to be within the letter of the constitution. This way of doing things would, the King thought, morally disarm the Duce's private army and remove any excuse for intervention by the Third Reich, since the matter would be purely domestic. That was the reason for the great importance that the prudent King attached to his relations with Grandi, who was to play an essential part in the process of undermining and wearing away the régime.

In the Fascist Grand Council, Count Grandi was supported in his rebellion by Ciano and Bottaï. The latter had just been ousted from the Ministry of Education. Even so, as has just been seen, Victor Emmanuel III had set himself the task not only of ridding himself of Mussolini as head of the government, but also of putting an end to the totalitarian régime that had been instituted in Italy following the "March on Rome" at the end of October 1922. Clearly he could not talk about this to the disgruntled Fascist ex-ministers. At the most, he thought he could work with them in the same way as Carboni.

△ *The Quirinal Palace, residence of King Victor Emmanuel III and one of the conspirators' headquarters.*

▽ *Victor Emmanuel Orlando, like Bonomi, was a previous Prime Minister disturbed by Italy's constant reverses, not only at the hands of the Allies but of Germany as well.*

In his plans to overthrow the régime, the King spoke to prime ministers of the Liberal era such as Victor Emmanuel Orlando and Ivanoë Bonomi in private audiences at the Quirinal Palace. But both were in their eighties and had been away from public life for more than 20 years. Besides, the opportunity presented by some "military disaster", which would precipitate the movement, as Grandi mentioned to General Puntoni after his audience with the King on February 12, was a great deal more difficult to seize than he had somewhat lightly imagined.

German reinforcements for Italy

With every fresh defeat suffered by Italian arms, several thousand more Germans crossed the Brenner Pass into Italy. Certainly, their primary task was to help in the defence of Corsica, Sardinia, Sicily, and southern Italy against landings which were expected from their mutual enemy. But German troops were sent also with the intention of preventing Italy from drawing the obvious conclusions from the increasingly hopeless strategic situation. The "whalebone stiffeners", as Hitler described German reinforcements, had become prison bars . . .

The position, however, was worse still. There is no doubt that the defeats foreseen by Grandi would remove the small amount of prestige that Mussolini still enjoyed among the Italian people. At the same time they would bring about the destruction of those military forces on which, in the event of an armistice following Mussolini's downfall, the new régime was counting to oppose, if it became necessary, the ever-growing number of German troops in Italy. It is thus easier to understand, though General Carboni in his memoirs does not, the fears which held General Ambrosio, Cavallero's successor as head of *Comando Supremo*, while he awaited Italy's change of course, as dangerous as it was vital.

The situation grew more serious as the gradual reinforcement of the Wehrmacht in Italy gave Hitler a multitude of pretexts for infiltrating hundreds of secret agents into the country and for recruiting generously-paid informers from the highest level of the State administration and the Fascist hierarchy. *Wilhelmstrasse* archives demonstrate quite clearly that some of the Duce's closest associates did not hesitate to report to Mackensen on the secret debates of the Italian Cabinet.

Was Mussolini unaware of these dealings? Was he also ignorant of the web being spun between the Royal Palace, the Army, and the opposition wing in his own party, in order to oust him from power? It is difficult to believe that he was. Yet, after the reaction marked by the "Changing of the Guard" on February 5, his behaviour between that date and the famous session of July 25, 1943, was characterised by a strange apathy.

Some remarks by Mussolini's wife are pertinent at this point.

"Two months before the Allied landings in Sicily, a lady of the Court informed me that secret meetings aimed at overthrowing my husband were being held at Castelporziano. The leaders of the plot were Grandi, Bottaï, and Federzoni, but the person who held the strings was none other than our cousin Badoglio, who intended to sacrifice not only Mussolini but the King and the dynasty as well.

"From what I have been told, Galeazzo [Ciano] was also in the plot. And yet my husband held him in great respect and appreciated his quick intelligence. Nevertheless he reproached him for allowing himself to be influenced by certain sectors of the Roman aristocracy that Benito and I had always avoided. I, for my part, was well aware of my son-in-law's opinion of me. He thought I was too *petit-bourgeois* and down-to-earth. On my side I certainly could not approve of his uncontrolled ambition and his liking for golf courses and society gatherings."